W9-CPB-480

New Wood
Puzzle Designs

New Wood Puzzle Designs

A Guide to the Construction of Both New and Historic Puzzles

James W. Follette, M.D.

LINDEN PUBLISHING
FRESNO, CA

New Wood Puzzle Designs

ISBN 0-941936-57-0

First Printing: September 2001
Printed in Singapore

Acknowledgments:

Writing this book has been an interesting and rewarding experience. There are a number of people who have helped me with its development. Special thanks go out to:

Dave Freedman, my first editor at *American Woodworker*

Ellis Walentine, for selecting my puzzle to publish

Richard Sorsky, my publisher, for encouraging me to write this book

Jim Goold for beautiful drawings

Bob Mescavage for beautiful photography

Phil Brindisi for the x-ray

And of course to my wife, Carol, for her constant encouragement, and my kids, Kristin, Jamie, and Mike, for their patience, especially when I pushed them and their friends to play with my puzzles.

Library of Congress Cataloging-in-Publication Data

Follette, James, 1948 -
    New wood puzzle designs / by James Follette.
        p. cm.
    ISBN 0-941936-57-0 (pbk.)
    1. Wooden toy making. 2. Puzzles. I . Title.

TT174.5.w6 F6525 2001
745.592--dc21

2001050193

LINDEN PUBLISHING

*The Woodworker's
Library*

LINDEN PUBLISHING INC.
2006 S. MARY ST.
FRESNO, CA 93721 USA
TEL 800-345-4447
WWW.LINDENPUB.COM

Table of Contents

Introduction

I have enjoyed playing with puzzles since I was a child. I can still remember the plastic "Howdy Doody" that disassembled into multiple pieces. Then there was the plastic sliding puzzle with pieces numbered 1 through 24 that could be solved, after frustration set in, by popping the pieces out of the case and pressing them back in, in order. I remember wire puzzles and tangrams, jigsaw puzzles and stacking puzzles. Puzzles were an important part of my youth, and their allure has remained with me ever since.

My Dad enjoyed woodworking and his obvious delight when working in his shop rubbed off on me. He introduced me to his almost antique, no-name scroll saw when I was about ten. He gave me some instruction, but more important, he gave me the freedom to experiment. He taught me to work safely, and also encouraged me to create. My free time and pocketbook haven't been the same since.

My wife, Carol, really encouraged my puzzle designing and making. About ten years ago she gave me a copy of *Puzzles Old and New* by Slocum and Botermans. (See the Bibliography. Unfortunately, this book is out of print, but it's possible to obtain copies from used book dealers.) I consider this book a puzzle bible, and it really stimulated my interest. Also, at Christmastime, Carol was happy to sell my puzzles in the gift store that she owned.

Puzzle making became my inroad to a delightful relationship with our local woodworking group. It has been a wonderful experience to be associated with the men and women of The Northeast Woodworkers Association. NWA was started by nine retired GE engineers in a living room in 1991, and as I write this (in early 2001), there are more than 700 members. Each year the annual "Expo" is an opportunity for members to display their work, to sell their work, and to enter their work in a competition judged by woodworking professionals. In 1997, a puzzle I had made won first place in its division. Ellis Walentine, at the time the editor of *American Woodworker* magazine, was one of the judges. As a result of that connection, one of my puzzles was published in that magazine in August 1998. As a result of that article I was asked to write this book. You just never know where puzzle making might lead.

So...I enjoy puzzles and I enjoy woodworking. These are some of the other things that attract me to making puzzles:

Many puzzles can be made in a short amount of time. While I do enjoy making furniture, I anticipate most of those projects will take me days or weeks to complete (unlike Norm Abrams, who, in his *New Yankee Workshop*, can turn out an attractive, elaborate piece of furniture in a half-hour on a Saturday morning!). With puzzles we are talking hours, if you don't include the time it takes for glue to dry and finish to set.

Since most puzzles are small, they can be made from scraps left over from other projects. You can also make lots of puzzle parts from the assorted, inexpensive "offcuts" available at most lumber mills. When I choose to splurge on the "good stuff," such as zebrawood, padauk, or wenge, I get to make a lot of puzzles for my buck.

Puzzles make nice gifts.

Puzzles sell well at craft fairs and woodworking shows. My booth has always attracted lots of attention, and I always have samples of different puzzles available for people to play with. Although I would not anticipate making a fortune, it is possible to have the hobby (almost) pay for itself. (Remember, the typical craft-fair attendee doesn't usually appreciate that cocobolo has to sell for more than stained pine.)

There are a lot of other puzzlers out there and it is fun to network with them. For example, an article on my hexagonal dovetail puzzle was published with my e-mail address at the end, and as a result I received hundreds of messages from the U.S. and around the world. This communication has been one of the most rewarding aspects of my puzzle work.

What might this book become for you?

A source of puzzle designs, with descriptions of my approach to construction. I have also provided solutions to many of the puzzles so that you can solve them after you make them.

An impetus not only to try making the puzzles described herein, but also to try creating new puzzles based on the ideas in this book. I hope I can get your creative juices flowing, and I would love for you to tell me about your ideas when you are done.

A collection of woodworking tips based on what I have learned through trial and error.

A reference on dealing with injuries in the workshop. As a physician, this is, of course, an area of significant interest to me. You might not expect to find this information in a book about building puzzles, but if I can help you avoid injuries, then I am practicing good preventative medicine.

Okay, let's get started. Good luck and have fun! For more puzzle information, check out my web site, www.docjimspuzzles.com; if you have questions or comments, feel free to e-mail me at jim@docjimspuzzles.com

Jim Follette
August 2001

Dedication:

To Carol, my Honey Bunny, who makes finding happiness in life much less of a puzzle.

CHAPTER 1

Thoughts on wood, glue, sanding, and finishes

Intelligent puzzle making involves more than just cutting wood into suitable shapes. Even with an appropriate plan on paper or in mind, there are other considerations in creating beautiful, functional, long-lasting puzzles. These include choices of woods, glue, sanding approaches, and finish.

Wood, the gift

I love wood. I love walking through stacks of boards. I love making my selections and carrying them to my workshop (stopping, of course, at the register on the way). I love the look, feel, smell, touch, and, especially, the potential of wood boards. Many times I will buy a variety of pieces of wood without specific projects in mind just to have that potential in my shop.

In my opinion, wood is a gift available to us for our intelligent use. When I work with wood it is in my consciousness, or not far beneath it, that there was life there. I try to use my skill to create something that will reflect my respect for that life. If I create something, such as a puzzle, that someone will admire for its beauty and grace, handle for its texture and warmth, and play with for its challenge, then I have continued the circle. I have expressed my appreciation for the gift.

One other point: I purchase exotic hardwoods solely from retailers who buy from suppliers belonging to organizations, such as the Tropical Forest Foundation, that promote the environmentally conscientious harvest of tropical woods. It is only the healthy future of the earth and existing wood species that are at stake.

The structure of wood

When I started making puzzles, especially more complex puzzles, I had a lot of failures. Glued joints didn't hold. Interlocking puzzles worked smoothly only in the winter. Balls got stuck in the ball mazes. Fortunately, most of the failures happened with puzzles I was making for my own enjoyment, before I started selling them or giving them away. What really helped me to deal with some of these problems was to get a better understanding of wood. Much of what I have learned is from Bruce Hoadley's great book *Understanding Wood* and from publications of the Forest Products Laboratory of the U.S. Forest Service. See the Bibliography for details on these.

I will summarize some of the important points here.

Wood is the skeletal remains of a tree. When the cells of the tree die and decompose, what is left behind are cell walls and mostly empty space between the walls. The cell walls are made up of three major components: cellulose, hemicelluloses, and lignin. Celluloses and hemicelluloses, which for simplicity's sake I will refer to from now on as cellulose, are complex polymers composed of sugar molecules. (Here's a trivia question: How come termites can use wood for food and humans can't? Answer: Because termite guts contain bacteria or protozoa, which break cellulose down into simple sugars, and human digestive systems don't.) The polymers of cellulose exist as long chains and crystalline clumps. The lignin is like a glue that holds the chains and clumps together. Now, and this is one of the most important parts of the story, even after the tree is dead the cellulose continues to interact with the environment, especially the water vapor in the environment. There are certain parts of the sugar molecules that attract and grab water molecules or glue molecules or finish molecules. When water attaches (binds) to these sites, the cellulose changes shape. Adding water makes cell walls fatter, removing water makes cell walls shrink.

There are other components contained by the wood, called extractives. These components are called extractives because they are extracted by solvents such as water, alcohol, and acetone. Extractives consist of elements such as oils, waxes, resins, and colorants, and influence properties like color, odor, density, and the ability of water to move into and out of the cell walls.

So, for me at least, learning about wood and trying to think in molecular terms has increased my understanding of some of the larger concepts and how they relate to puzzle making.

Wood and moisture/movement

As I have just said, even though it is "dead," wood continues to interact with water in the environment, swelling and shrinking depending on the moisture content of the wood relative to the humidity in the air. In other words, wood is hygroscopic. There are many properties of wood that affect hygroscopicity. One of these, as mentioned, is the presence of certain types of extractives. Some extractives are oily or waxy and resist water movement in and out of the wood. Species of woods with lots of this type of extractive, such as teak and rosewood, are very stable with regard to moisture-related movement. Woods like these are great for making puzzle pieces—as long as they don't have to be glued together, at least not with water-based glues.

Another property that has an effect on movement is density. Wood density, simply put, though not entirely the whole story, is a reflection of the thickness of the cell walls, and therefore the amount of cellulose that is packed in. The denser the wood, the more sugars. The more sugars, the more binding sites for water to attach to. "Not entirely" refers to the fact that there are many dense woods, especially tropical hardwoods, which are moisture-stable because of the presence of water-resisting extractives. Examples of denser

My Preferred Puzzle Woods

I love wood and I could go on for pages describing the qualities I like about this species and what I don't like about that species. Let me cut to the chase. I have selected four woods that I have developed a particular preference for in my puzzle making, and I will tell you the reasons why.

For puzzle pieces that do not require gluing, I like Brazilian rosewood. Although it doesn't machine as well as some other species, and it tends to be a bit brittle, it does take on a smooth surface with minimal effort. Its extractives make it moisture-stable and create color patterns that I find attractive. It's becoming rare, however, and is expensive.

Another colorful tropical hardwood I like is padauk. The red color is attractive in many different puzzle applications, but it is important to note that this red will fade to brownish black over time when exposed to sunlight. The wood is easy to machine, though its dust can be irritating. It is moisture-stable and glues well. One concern when finishing padauk: The red-colored extractives will dissolve in some finish solvents and bleed into surrounding woods. This seems to be a problem with highly aromatic solvents. Padauk seems to be readily available from my usual suppliers.

My favorite domestic hardwood is black walnut. Its dark chocolate color and easy workability make it very attractive to me. It is less moisture-stable than many other woods, but it does glue up well. It is readily available and reasonably priced.

My all around favorite woods for puzzle making are American and Honduran mahogany. I find mahogany easy to work and, because of its fine grain, it smoothes with little effort. It is reasonably moisture-stable and glues well. Its color continues to evolve over time into a magnificent reddish-brown. I have read that mahogany is becoming scarce and, therefore, more expensive. I hope that appropriate forest management techniques will keep this wonderful wood available in an increasing supply.

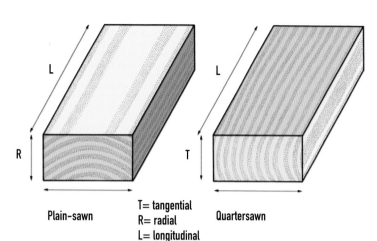

Plain-sawn

T = tangential
R = radial
L = longitudinal

Quartersawn

woods that are less moisture-stable include hickory and maple. Examples of dense woods that are more stable because of extractives include teak and rosewood. Also, with regard to density, there are other considerations. While dense woods tend to be stronger, which is a good thing, denser woods tend to dull sharp tools more quickly, a bad thing.

Moisture-related wood movement is not uniform, making it even harder to accommodate. The movement is anisotropic, that is, wood swells and shrinks in differing amounts in relation to the growth rings. Wood movement is greatest tangential to the growth rings. There is less movement radially, or across the growth rings, and least movement longitudinally, or perpendicular to the growth rings (that is, the long dimension of the board). In fact, for most woods, tangential movement is 1-1/2 to 3-1/2 times greater than radial movement. This explains, for example, why quartersawn boards are more stable than plain-sawn wood. With quartersawn boards, most movement occurs in the smallest dimension, which is the board's thickness.

Stability in Wood

Of the many reasons for selecting a specific wood for a particular puzzle project, stability with respect to moisture is high on the list. This is especially true for interlocking puzzles where a tight fit is necessary. Stewart Coffin, who is one of the greatest American puzzle makers and a specialist in interlocking puzzles, researched this issue. He took blocks of various wood and measured them at different times of the year in his workshop in Massachusetts. The following evaluation of wood stability is from his book *Puzzle Craft*.

Best – cocobolo, padauk, teak, African blackwood

Very good – Brazilian rosewood, tulipwood, ebony, breadnut

Good – Honduras mahogany, koa, limba, primavera, satinwood

Fair – ash, walnut, bubinga

Poor – birch, cherry, maple, beech, hickory, oak

Coping with wood movement

Accepting the fact that wood is going to move, can things be done to minimize the effect on puzzles? In Understanding Wood, Bruce Hoadley describes five ways for coping with wood movement. They include
- preshrinking
- atmospheric control
- mechanical restraint
- chemical stabilization
- design

Preshrinking—Living trees are loaded with water. After a tree is felled, the wood shrinks as the water departs. Allowing the wood to dry to a moisture content that is in equilibrium with the moisture content of the air around it (called equilibrium moisture content or EMC), can take one to two years. The length of time depends on the thickness of the wood, the air flow around the wood, and the temperature and relative humidity of the air. (Relative humidity is a measure of moisture content of the air—the actual humidity divided by the total humidity that the air can hold at that temperature.) Drying can be hastened by heating the wood in a kiln. Regardless of whether the wood has been kiln-dried or air-dried, I usually allow all wood I buy to rest in my workshop for a few weeks so that it can acclimate to ambient conditions.

Atmospheric control—In the home shop, you can control the moisture of the air around your wood with air conditioners, humidifiers, and dehumidifiers. On a smaller scale, for special puzzles, you can make a relatively airtight case and increase or decrease moisture as needed with the use of desiccants, a technique used with cigar humidors. In addition, you can control moisture gain and loss to some extent by applying a finish to the wood (more on this to follow). And here's a trick that has actually worked for me: Make puzzles with interlocking pieces that fit fairly tightly in the spring and fall, when wood is midway between winter and summer moisture content.

Mechanical restraint—In some applications (which usually don't come into play with puzzlemaking), wood movement is controlled by restraining the pieces with metal straps. Movement can also be minimized by using plywood, which is made by gluing together an odd number of wood layers. The plywood is assembled with the grain of each layer running opposite to the grain of the adjacent layers, so it is inherently more stable than solid wood. In jigsaw puzzles, plywood can be a most useful medium.

Chemical stabilization—Two chemicals are typically used to stabilize wood: propylene glycol and methylmethacrylate. Processes exist in which the water-binding sites of cellulose are chemically altered, such as with acetylation, to make them more moisture-resistant. I have no experience with these to pass along.

Design—With some puzzles, design modifications can be made to accommodate wood movement. I describe one such approach when talking about the lighthouse ball maze puzzle (shown on pg. 35). With some puzzles, though, there is no way to modify the design. One thing that well-known puzzle maker Stewart Coffin does is to have the grain of all the pieces of an interlocking puzzle run in the same direction. This, he says, tends to cancel out the effect of the movement of any individual piece.

Let me summarize some of what I've presented so far in dealing with wood movement with reference to my puzzle making.

I try to choose wood that is moisture-stable, especially when making puzzle pieces that have to fit tightly with other pieces.

I pay attention to grain orientation. This helps me predict in which direction most movement will be expected.

I allow wood to acclimate to my shop environment for at least several weeks before using it in puzzle making.

When I create puzzles, part of my challenge may be to incorporate design features that compensate for wood movement.

My Preferred Puzzle Glues

My dad, with a little bit of my help, built me a small boat, a pram, in our basement back in 1962. One of the things I remember was having to mix the glue, a small quantity at a time, as we went along. It was tedious. One thing I took from that experience is that I now have a preference for glues that are convenient to use.

Most of the time I stick with yellow glue, also called modified PVA glue. I find it produces a good joint when mating surfaces make good contact without gaps, sawdust, dirt, extractives, or finish in the way. Conditions under which the glue hardens are not stringent, but unusual extremes of temperature, say, below 50 degrees or above 85 degrees, result in poor joints. Lower temperatures result in "chalky" joints, which don't hold well. Reasonable joints can be produced when clamping is not possible by applying glue to the joint and rubbing the wood pieces back and forth with some pressure until there is resistance to sliding. This action seems to push glue below the surfaces somewhat.

Squeeze-out of this glue onto the wood next to the joint, or even small amounts of glue dripped or finger-smudged onto the wood, will prevent penetration of stain or finish. Cleaning up glue goofs isn't easy, and wiping with a moist rag just spreads the glue around. What I have done occasionally when I have decided to prefinish puzzle parts, is to mask off the areas to be glued with masking tape before applying the finish. Any excess glue can then be easily removed.

I have used polyurethane glue in some limited applications. Again, surfaces to be joined must be smooth and free of dust and finish. Polyurethane glue has almost no tack (stickiness when first applied), and pieces tend to slide during clamping. And clamps must be applied, which may be difficult with small, irregular pieces. Since polyurethane glue expands as it cures (hopefully into the cell spaces and cell walls), if the pieces are not held tightly together, the glue will actually push them apart. One good thing is that glue squeeze-out from joints forms a foam that is easy to remove and doesn't affect the stainability or finishability of the wood it touches.

Glue

Many of my puzzles require that parts be glued together. This can become quite challenging because the area of contact between pieces can be extremely small. An understanding of how glue works and how to best prepare wood surfaces for gluing will help you achieve strong, long-lasting glue joints.

Glue holds materials together in two ways. The first way is called interlocking action or mechanical adhesion. In this case, glue in liquid form penetrates the nooks and crannies of the wood, into cell cavities and into and around cell walls, and anchors itself during solidification. The second way glue works is by valence forces, also called specific adhesion. Valence forces are the attractions between the molecules, atoms, and ions of the glue and the wood. (In simplistic terms, think of the interlocking action as your fingers intertwine—valence forces would be like interlocking your fingers while wearing Velcro gloves.) In order to form a strong joint, the glue must penetrate into sound wood two to six cell layers deep.

Here are some tips that will help you to construct sound glue joints.

The two wood surfaces should mate as snugly as possible. Does it go without saying that making perfectly mating pieces of perfect dimension is the first goal of woodworking? There are glues that can be used with good success when there is space between the surfaces, epoxy for example. But glues such as polyvinyl acetate or PVA (white glue), modified PVA (yellow glue), and polyurethane form the strongest bond when there is only a thin film of glue and no air space between the wood surfaces, since pockets of trapped air prevent bonding. Thicker layers of PVA glues (yellow and white glues), don't polymerize as well as thinner layers; because they are water-based glues, they contract as the water evaporates, making it less likely that the glue film will span the gap. Polyurethane glue releases bubbles of carbon dioxide, which make the glue foam as it cures. When controlled, this glue foam expands into the wood layers, increasing the amount of interlock and valence force. But if the material expands in the space between poorly mating surfaces, the glue-foam actually results in a weak joint.

Each surface should be free of irregularities such as saw- or planer-blade marks. Cell walls should be cleanly severed, not crushed, to keep the cell cavities and spaces around cell walls open so that glue can pass through to deeper layers of the wood. This requires sharp blades and sharp sandpaper. I find that for small pieces sandpaper finer than 100 grit (I prefer sanding stepwise up to 220) provides the best cell wall cleavage without introducing surface irregularities. Sandpaper finer than 320 can produce wood dust so fine that it will clog spaces between cell layers and may be difficult to vacuum out or remove with a tack cloth. Use this grade of sandpaper to prepare the wood for finishing, not gluing.

Gluing surfaces should be free of burnishes, dirt, and extractives (waxes, oils, and resins). Anything that prevents the penetration of the glue into the wood will interfere with the soundness of the joint. In addition, pieces are best glued within 24 hours of preparation. When you prepared the wood for gluing, you removed extractives, and they can re-accumulate over time and affect the integrity

---

Ease of Gluing

This table is derived from a Forest Products Laboratory publication. It categorizes wood species according to ease of bonding. These are generalizations and reflect use of various types of glue.

Bonds easily	Bonds well	Bonds satisfactorily	Bonds with difficulty
Aspen	Butternut	Ash	Osage-orange
Basswood	Maple, soft	Birch	Teak
Chestnut	Black walnut	Cherry	Rosewood
Purpleheart	Mahogany	Maple, hard	
	Philippine	Oak	
	American	Red	
		White	
		Bubinga	

If you compare this list with the list of stable woods generated by Coffin (pg. 12), there are a few interesting conclusions. Many woods that are moisture-stable do not glue well. They are better for puzzles in which gluing isn't necessary. Others glue well but are moisture-unstable. This makes better sense when you remember the molecular structure of wood (pg. 10).

of the glue joint. Also, if you put off gluing, the wood surfaces may distort in response to changing moisture conditions. The last step before glue application—vacuuming or using a tack cloth—will remove residual sawdust and other debris from the surface.

There is extensive research indicating that wood extractives can prevent good glue penetration. Some extractives, such as those in teak and Brazilian rosewood, repel water, so water-based glues won't penetrate well. Some people report success using epoxy or polyurethane glue with wood containing water-repelling extractives. I typically don't use these types of wood for puzzles that will require strong glue joints. A good test of the ability of water-based glues to penetrate is this: Drop a bead of water on the wood, and if it doesn't start to spread out in 30 seconds, the glue likely won't penetrate well.

There are just a few other things to consider when gluing, such as the direction of the grain. Glue applied to end grain typically is absorbed too deeply, which decreases the amount of glue on the surface and weakens the joint. Side-grain to side-grain gluing is strongest, but with dense wood glue may have difficulty penetrating to a depth of a few cell layers. With any type of wood, clamping is important to force glue into the deeper layers, but good clamping is absolutely essential for dense wood—clamping pressure of 250 to 300 pounds per square inch is typically recommended. This is easily achieved with c-clamps, bar clamps, or other clamps with screw-type mechanisms. Notice that spring clamps are not on the list.

The qualities of a particular glue are important as well. Glue has a tendency to thicken when exposed to the air. This is typical of glue sitting in a bottle half-filled with air on a shelf. Once thickened, the glue won't penetrate as well and thus the bond will be weak. Also, because all wood moves some with changes in humidity, cured glue must have a certain amount of flexibility to accommodate this movement or the joint will fail.

Sanding

As we've already discussed to some extent, there are four aspects of surface condition that are important in achieving a high-quality wood finish. They are trueness, evenness, smoothness, and quality of the cell walls of the wood. Trueness is a measure of how the actual geometry of the surface compares to its intended geometry. Evenness refers to the smooth mating of joints. Smoothness implies the absence of irregularities, such as planer-blade undulations and tear-outs. The quality of the cell walls deals with whether the wood was cut cleanly with sharp tools or crushed into shape with dull tools. (Here again, knowledge of the molecular structure of wood helps build an understanding of what is happening here.) Sanding is an important step in every one of these categories.

One of the best things that can be said about sanding puzzles is that puzzles tend to be small and irregular, and surface imperfections prior to finish application have less of an overall impact than, for example, they would on a dining-table top. One of the worst things about sanding puzzles is that the pieces tend to be small and irregular, require a lot of hand work, and frequently require tedious precision-sanding to fit together properly. As you might have guessed, sanding is not my favorite aspect of puzzle making. Although I know proper sanding is necessary to turn out attractive puzzles, I find it quite boring. That said, let me tell you how I handle this task and what I do to beat the boredom.

When sanding large pieces, I usually start with 80-grit paper on my bench-top sander, oscillating spindle sander, or 1-inch belt sander. Then I move to 120 grit. Next, I sand with my vibrating palm sander using 150- and 180-grit papers. I usually finish with 220 grit, sanding by hand. With small pieces where I have to sand almost everything by hand, I usually start with 120-grit paper or finer. Whatever the size of the puzzle parts, using sandpaper of increasingly smaller grits in a stepwise fashion saves work in the long run by eliminating the sanding scratches that could mar the final product.

Up to this stage the sandpaper, belts, or drums I prefer are open-coat aluminum oxide. This is because the aluminum-oxide particles tend to fracture into smaller—but still sharp—pieces as they are used rather than wear down. The particles stay sharper longer, and are therefore more likely to cleave cellulose pieces rather than to crush them. Because open-coat papers have spaces between the abrasive particles, debris can accumulate between the particles without compromising the effectiveness of the paper.

During the next step, I raise the grain with a gentle mist of water mixed with rubbing alcohol from a spray bottle, then sand again with 220 grit. Two things about this: I think the alcohol helps the water evaporate more quickly, and I don't bother to do this with species such as rosewood because the water doesn't penetrate well.

At this point, I sometimes take the optional step of giving the piece a sanding with 220-grit up to 320-grit garnet paper. Why?

My Preferred Puzzle Finishes

Up front I will say that I am still searching for the perfect finish for my puzzles. I don't think it exists yet. So I will share what I use now.

On many interlocking puzzles I use something I found in a hardware store called "beeswax in lemon oil." It is really sold as a furniture polish. It consists of a lemon-scented drying oil (I doubt if it comes from lemon trees), and a medium-hardness wax (which is probably not from bees). I use it because it is easy to apply, easy to reapply, is enhanced by the oil from peoples' hands when they play with the puzzles, and, when rubbed out, produces a satin luster. It also allows the puzzle pieces to slide against each other easily.

For non-interlocking puzzles, I usually wipe on a coat of tung oil and follow that with three coats of gel polyurethane. I rub the wood with an abrasive polyester pad between each coat. For puzzles made of disks, which can be turned on the drill press, I apply finish as the disks spin. I use something called "Woodturner's Finish," which I think is a rapid-drying varnish. It could be a lacquer, but the label doesn't say. All I know is that I have found it does what I want it to do.

For puzzles that require gluing, I usually wait until after complete assembly before applying finish, although sometimes I choose to prefinish puzzle parts. (In this case I mask off the areas to be glued with masking tape, so the finish won't get in the way of penetration of the glue.) It would be nice to routinely be able to apply finish to small pieces before gluing, but that would require an uncommon glue. Think about it in molecular terms. Glues work by attaching around and to cellulose molecules, and one of a finish's jobs is to prevent anything from getting to those cellulose molecules.

Garnet is softer than aluminum oxide and wears down into smooth clumps rather than fracturing into sharp particles. Although I don't know for sure, I suspect that the garnet paper flattens the microscopic irregularities in the clumps of cellulose that have been cleaved by "burnishing" them or bending them over. Another thing is that the grooves dug by garnet paper tend to be U-shaped, while those left by aluminum oxide, because of the sharper particles, are V-shaped. Surface finishes such as polyurethane more easily fill U-shaped grooves, resulting in a smoother finish.

Finally comes the finish. Between coats of finish, especially polyurethane, I rub with a special polyester rubbing pad that has abrasive bound to it. I used to use steel wool for this but the polyester pads don't fragment.

Later I describe turning wooden disks on the drill press and sanding them by hand with a length of sanding belt or folded sandpaper as they spin. When I do this, I move up the progressions of sandpaper grits that I have described.

As a last note, remember always to sand along the grain, since grooves left by along-the-grain sanding tend to blend in with the grain. Sanding across the grain leaves grooves that require work to smooth out. While it's useful for removing lots of wood fast, this is usually not an issue with puzzle parts.

Now let's talk about fighting boredom. Here's what works for me. In my basement near my shop I have a TV and an old easy chair. I take a box of puzzle pieces that need hand-sanding, a bunch of sandpaper, a cup of coffee, turn on the TV, sit in the easy chair, and have at it. This is one time when concentrating on woodworking as you're doing it is the opposite of necessary.

Wood finishes

The worst nightmare (so far) in my puzzle career had to do with finish. Several years ago I was selling puzzles at an outdoor craft fair over a July weekend. My booth was inside a tent, and the conditions inside were even hotter and more humid than outside. I had a number of wooden puzzles for sale, including a few of the interlocking variety. I had made most of the puzzles during the month preceding the fair and had experimented with a new finish—shellac, I think. On Sunday morning, one of Saturday's customers returned to my booth with one of the interlocking puzzles he had bought. "Boy," he said, "this puzzle sure is great. I can't figure out how to make even the first piece move to start solving it. Can you give me a hint?"

Well, I couldn't get the first piece to move either, and I knew how to solve it. The puzzle was sticky, not tricky. It was stuck together as tightly as if I had finished it with glue, which, in fact, was kind of what I had done. I quickly gave the customer a new unstuck puzzle and an extra one for his trouble.

What I didn't know then is that shellac is thermolabile, meaning that it is unstable when it's heated. Apparently the shellac had softened in the heat, flowed from piece to piece, and solidified when it cooled down.

In this section, I'll try to relate some of the other useful things I have learned since that craft fair about finish.

In his informative book, *The New Wood Finishing Book*, author Michael Dresdner defines the following functions of a finish: to protect wood from scratches, dirt, stains, and wear; to enhance the natural beauty, color, figure, grain, and depth of the wood; to preserve wood from water, oxidation, and, ultraviolet rays; and to change the wood's appearance

Moisture-Fighting Finishes

The Forest Products Laboratory of the Forest Service of the U.S. Department of Agriculture is an excellent source of information for woodworkers. Much of the information derived from investigations at its facility, as well as information from other sources, is available on the website www.fpl.fs.fed.us. The following is derived from an FPL publication entitled "Protecting Wood From Humidity," and from an article of the same name by Feist and Peterson in the May/June 1987 issue of *Fine Woodworking* magazine. Obviously, some of the finishes tested are not appropriate for puzzle use, but the results are interesting nonetheless.

The moisture-excluding effectiveness (MEE) of three coats of finish, when pieces of wood were exposed to 14 days of 90-percent relative humidity at 80 degrees, were reported as follows:

Finish	MEE
Melted paraffin wax (one coat, dipped)	95
Two-component epoxy/polyamide gloss paint	87
Aluminum-pigmented polyurethane gloss varnish	84
Soya-tung satin enamel	80
Pigmented flat shellac	73
Two-component polyurethane wood sealer	63
Orange or white shellac	46
Phenolic/tung floor sealer	35
Acrylic gloss latex varnish	10
Tung oil	2
Paste wax	1
Linseed oil	0
Spray furniture polish/lemon oil	0

by adding color and hiding defects. With respect to wooden puzzles, I would also add another function: the ability to provide smoothness and/or lubrication to allow pieces to move easily against one another. Most important with regard to tight-fitting puzzle pieces, though, is attempting to retard the movement of moisture in and out of the wood. It is important to realize that no finish can totally prevent movement—the best any finish can do is to slow movement down. You can see how some popular finishes stack up in the sidebar on the previous page.

Ultimately, finish choice is a matter of personal preference. If you like the way a particular finish makes your puzzle look, feel, or function, use that finish by all means. Still, some experimentation is warranted, since all finishes offer different qualities. Here are some things to keep in mind.

Finishes can be separated into two groups—penetrating and non-penetrating. Penetrating finishes are typically based on oils derived from plants. They sink into the wood to a few cell layers deep, and flow in and around the cellulose. Then they dry, at least somewhat. Penetrating finishes tend not to leave much of themselves on the surface of the wood. Examples of penetrating finishes are linseed, tung, and walnut oils. Some people call them drying oils, to distinguish them from oils that don't dry, like mineral oil. As can be seen from the sidebar on the previous page, penetrating finishes are not good at reducing moisture movement.

Non-penetrating, or coating, finishes, may sink in a little but they really work by forming a protective covering on the wood surface. Examples of these finishes are shellac, lacquer, wax, and polyurethane. As can be seen, some of these provide moderate moisture protection.

Here are some other helpful ways to categorize finishes.

Evaporative or reactive: These terms refer to the way in which a surface coating is formed on the wood. Evaporative finishes, such as wax, shellac, and lacquer, do not change chemically as their solvents evaporate. They will re-dissolve in their original solvent, or in others. Evaporative finishes tend to be softer than reactive finishes

On Varnishes, Oils, and Resins

Varnish is a generic term that many people use to refer to any clear finish for wood, but I prefer to use it more selectively. Varnishes consist of two components: a vegetable oil—usually linseed, soybean, or tung—and a modifying resin. The oil holds the resin in suspension; as the oil dries, the resin is exposed to oxygen and polymerizes into a large (large in molecular terms, that is) hardened film. By changing the ratio of oil to resin, it's possible to change the depth of penetration into the wood. For example, wiping oils such as Danish oil are about 75 percent oil and 25 percent resin, whereas surface coatings, such as polyurethane, may be from 40 to 50 percent oil.

Another way that the characteristics of varnish are changed is by using different resins. For example, the resin in polyurethane is toluene diisocyanate. Spar varnish, a finish whose popularity grew from its early use in shipbuilding, is a mix of phenolic resin and tung oil.

and are more likely to be affected by heat (meaning they are thermo-labile). Varnishes, by contrast, are reactive finishes. As noted in the sidebar on the preceding page, the polymerization, or curing, of the resin results in a new molecule that will not re-dissolve in the original solvent. In general, reactive finishes are tougher and more heat-stable than evaporative types. Compared to evaporative finishes, though, the application of reactive finishes may require more care and work. They may not layer out as smoothly during curing, they are more likely to trap air bubbles, and sanding may be necessary between coats.

Brush, spray, or wipe on: Some finishes, such as penetrating oils, wax, and the gel form of polyurethane, do well when wiped on with a rag. Others, such as lacquer and fast-drying varnish, may be best applied by spraying. Brushing is appropriate for most others. It is pretty obvious that wiping on with a rag requires less equipment and expertise than the other two methods.

Fast- or slow-drying: Some finishes, such as lacquer and shel-lac, dry quickly, in minutes. Some finishes, like linseed oil, take so long that they never seem to dry totally. Most finishes dry in hours. Catalysts, such as Japan driers, can be added to certain finishes to speed up the process. Water-soluble finishes tend to dry more quick-ly than solvent-based finishes.

Appearance: There are many ways to describe the appear-ances produced by various finishes. For example, oils add depth, or bring out "chatoyance," a term that refers to a type of glimmer or iri-descence that can be highlighted in various woods, such as mahogany, tiger maple, and lacewood. Another term is "luster," which refers to the ability of the surface to reflect or disperse light. Gloss, semi-gloss, satin, and flat are degrees of luster.

Additives: Chemicals can be added to finishes to incorporate or enhance certain desirable properties. A good example of this are the chemicals used to prevent ultraviolet light penetration. The color of some wood is changed over time by exposure to sunlight. To me, some changes are for the better. Mahogany and cherry, for example, become a deeper reddish-brown. Other changes are not so fortu-itous—padauk, for example, changes from red to blackish-brown and purpleheart goes from purple to brown. These changes can be held at bay by using finishes with added ultraviolet-light blockers.

CHAPTER 2

Workshop and tools

Before I discuss the tools that I've found invaluable in puzzle making, let me share my workshop rules:

Every new project is an excuse for a new tool.

You can never have enough clamps.

Always leave woodworking catalogs, with desired tools circled or otherwise well indicated, conspicuously around the house in December, May or June (for Mother's and Father's Day, respectively), and well in advance of your birthday.

You can never have enough sandpaper.

Buy a dust collector early in your woodworking career.

Buy quality products or you'll inevitably end up buying quantity (replacing and upgrading).

You can never have enough clean rags.

Inexpensive, good-quality used tools are better than cheap, poor-quality new tools.

Measure twice and cut once. (Or, as related by Douglas Whynott in *A Unit of Water, A Unit of Time*, a book about boat building, "Measure three times and cut once or measure twice and hammer to fit.")

Ten fingers at the start of the project, ten fingers at the end of the project.

A brief history of my shop tools

A Craftsman 10-inch table saw was the first tool that made me feel like I had a real workshop. Before my grandmother bought it for me in 1980, I did my work with power hand tools such as jigsaws and circular saws. With the table saw, I became more productive. Tables, shelves, and assorted other pieces looked better because they fit together more precisely. I recommend a table saw as the first major tool in any woodworking shop. I still use my Craftsman saw and will not part with it for sentimental reasons even though it has a lousy fence and is underpowered. I did buy a narrow-kerf, good-quality blade that helps the saw tremendously, but I still relegate it to rough-cutting. This saw came into my life while I was still in residency training, and my wife, kids, and I were living on a tight budget. My first major project, a bed, was made out of construction grade (#3 or worse) spruce. I decided then that I would consider myself financially successful in my career when I could afford to buy "good" wood.

Because of my interest in furniture making, a jointer/planer was my next purchase. With respect to puzzle making, it is excellent for making a sharp 90-degree angle between two sides of a wood stick. This is important for making precise cubes and rectangular solids, the application of which will be discussed later.

Next I bought a drill press that was marketed before current speed limits were enforced. It can turn at 8000 rpm, but I don't use it at that speed because of its tendency to become light on its pedestal and walk across the shop. Of course a drill press can drill reproducibly accurate holes, but it can also do lots more. I use mine to make disks and rings, as a vertical sander, and as a vertical lathe. With a mortising attachment, it does a reasonable job of cutting square holes.

I have subsequently added a radial arm saw, band saw, scroll saw, router and table, bench-top belt sander, and oscillating spindle sander to my shop, but the two tools that really improved my puzzle making were a thickness planer and a sliding compound miter saw. With these two tools I started experiencing real satisfaction in my ability to make precise puzzle pieces. The thickness planer lets me turn out multiple sticks of reproducibly accurate thickness and width—accuracy that is measurable with calipers! The sliding compound miter saw also offers great precision (for fun I've cut paper-thin slices from an 8/4, 6-inch-wide piece of black walnut). With a simple jig it's possible to manufacture innumerable pieces of exact length. Of course it's possible to perform the same operations accurately using other tools, but the ease my thickness planer and sliding compound miter saw provide more than justify their expense.

Shop safety

Familiarity with the capability of each of your tools and appreciation for your own ability to use your tools are critically important. The capabilities of most of the tools in my shop are fairly extensive, and even after a number of years I am still defining them. As far as my own abilities go, they have improved (I hope) over time, but vary by time of day, day of the week, etc. My major imperative is to try not to explore past the limits of safety. My tools have no conscience and will not shut off just because I try to do something intrinsically unsafe. Here are a few guidelines to help you develop—and keep—good habits of shop safety.

Read your tool manuals. If you buy a used tool that comes without a manual, contact the manufacturer for a replacement copy.

Use jigs or fixtures that put as much space as possible between you and the cutting edge. Attach small pieces of work to bigger pieces of stock for safer machining.

Remain physically balanced when in the shop. While working, stand so that changes in resistance against the piece being manipulated will not result in sudden shifts of your hands and fingers toward the cutter. Stand comfortably, and allow for occasional changes in position to avoid the stiffness and the loss of attention to work that can accompany a dull backache. Stand out of the line of fire of potential kickbacks.

Remain psychologically balanced as well. Don't work if you aren't able to fully concentrate on the work. Be careful with any substance that may have side effects, such as alcohol, pain medication, blood pressure medication, and so on. Many substances can impair judgment, but you won't realize it because your judgment is impaired. Be extremely careful if you are tired, angry, or hungry, and even more careful if you are in a hurry. Haste can lead to cutting corners, which can lead to cutting fingers.

Keep the shop floor as clean as possible. One tumble on a little piece of wood can send you head first into your workbench or worse.

Keep sawdust from accumulating, but if it does, be sure to keep cats out of the shop until you can clean up. (We have had more than one cat who thought sawdust was a lot like kitty litter.)

Keep offcuts away from the cutting area. They are prone to incidental contact with the cutter, which can result in UFOs (unpredictably flying objects).

Essential Tools for Those on A Limited Budget

Although many of the puzzles in this book require tools such as a drill press, a router with table, or a table saw, there are some puzzles that can be made with hand tools, such as the soma cubes in the next chapter. My recommendations for someone wanting to get started with puzzles but having limited financial resources to invest in tools would include the following: a hand miter saw (it cuts angles but also makes guided straight cuts), an electric hand drill, a fret saw, various clamps, wood chisels with a mallet, and sandpaper. For somebody with more money to spend, bench-top tools, usually smaller and less expensive additions of floor models, work very nicely in puzzle making, where pieces are typically small.

Think twice about disabling the safety features on shop tools. The most convenient way isn't always the safest way.

Think finesse, not force. Allow the blade, the bit, or the abrasive to work at its own pace.

CHAPTER 3

Puzzles from cubelets

Perfectly machined cubes are used to construct these puzzles. Featured are a soma cube (right), and two hidden cube ball mazes (center and left). A disassembled soma cube waits at center for the hands of a puzzle solver.

There are more than a few puzzles and games that can be made from cubelets. (I use the term cubelet to describe a small cube that is used to build larger cubes and other shapes.) Once the cubelets are made, all you have to do is glue them together. But precise puzzles require perfect cubelets, which require perfect sticks.

As Stewart Coffin says in his book, *Puzzle Craft*, "Making uniform, accurate, square sticks is ...essential for successful puzzle making. Careful attention to accuracy and uniformity at this stage will save trouble later on.... If your lumber is virtually free of warp, if you have a good table saw with a sharp blade of a type suitable for ripping and a long, straight rip fence, set up and adjusted just right, then perhaps you can rip out accurate square sticks in one operation. Usually not all of these conditions are met, and the alternative is to rip them out slightly oversized and plane them to exact size."

Perfectly square sticks

The goal in making perfectly square sticks is to create four sides at right angles to one another. It is possible to make a stick with opposite sides that are parallel but not square, and no matter how many times you run it through the thickness planer it will not become square. If you purchase wood with faces planed and one or two edges squared, always recheck the edges with a machinist's square to be sure the angle is 90 degrees for the length of the stick. If it isn't square, run the board across the jointer with the fence set at 90 degrees. Mark the side and newly created edge so you'll know after ripping the stick which sides are squared. The first run(s) through the thickness planer are done with the marked sides on the plate.

Square up sticks on the jointer before running them through the thickness planer.

Once the sticks are square, it's easy to cut them into perfect cubelets. I use the stick to set the stop on the miter saw. In this way the cubelets will be as long as they are wide. Be sure that the stick and cubelet remain flat on the table and square to the blade during the entire operation. If not, the cuts will not be straight, and/or the cubelet may become a UFO (unpredictably flying object). Cubelets can be made any size. I use mostly 1-inch cubelets in my puzzles, which means that I start with 5/4 wood or precisely milled 4/4 wood. Depending on preference, the cubelets can be made with lightly sanded edges, edges rounded by sanding, edges routed with a 1/8-inch round-over bit, or edges beveled with the table saw set at 45 degrees. The table saw can also be used to bevel the edges slightly or even to create a piece with 18 equal faces.

These cubelets feature a variety of edges that were either sanded or machined with a table saw. The wood shown here is American mahogany.

Soma cube

The soma cube, created by Piet Hein, is a very popular "non-interlocking assembly" puzzle. According to one source, the name "soma" was taken from Aldous Huxley's *Brave New World*. Soma was an addictive drug taken by inhabitants of the establishment to kill time. The soma cube is made from 27 cubelets. They may be identical or you can make 14 of one species and 13 of a contrasting species. The cubelets are glued to make seven shapes (polycubelets); six shapes have four cubes and one has three cubes, as shown on the next page. The polycubelets are stacked to make a cube and various other shapes. Many books and websites show the shapes that are possible to make with this puzzle. Check the Bibliography at the back of the book.

The soma puzzle contains seven components, each consisting of an assembly of cubelets. In this puzzle, the wood is oak dyed red and blue with aniline dye.

Cube Ball Maze

Here are two cube ball mazes, one made from oak, left, and the other from cherry and padauk, right.

By drilling holes in cubelets and assembling them to allow passage of a steel ball (I use a ball bearing), it is possible to create a challenging ball maze. The first step is to design a passage through the cube such as the one shown below. Using this as a guide, drill holes as indicated. Carefully glue the cubelets together so as not to obstruct the holes with glue. I create one layer at a time. The object is to pass the ball from one hole to the other by shifting the cube. It is primarily a matter of luck to get the ball through the maze.

I have found that in this puzzle, a hole measuring 1/16 inch larger than the ball provides adequate clearance. I use a 7/16-inch steel ball and a 1/2-inch metal/wood bit that has a standard 118-degree bevel, so that there is a smooth transition between holes that meet at 90 degrees. Each of the holes is drilled to a depth of 3/4 inch.

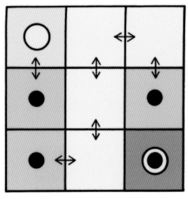

Top level

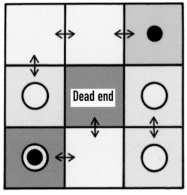

Middle level

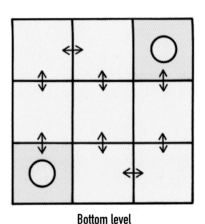

Bottom level

Hole in upper face

Hole in lower face

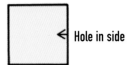

Hole in side

In a cube ball maze, each of the cubelets contains at least one drilled hole. When assembled into a cube, the holes form a maze for a ball to pass through. These figures represent a diagram you can use to construct a ball maze.

Pentominoes

Using five cubelets connected together in one plane, it is possible to make twelve different shapes. Solomon Golomb, who coined the term for combinations of multiple cubelets in his book, *Polyominoes*, discusses pentominoes as only a mathematician can. These twelve shapes can be made into many larger structures. Many of these shapes, along with solutions, can be found in different books and on websites. (See the Bibliography at the back of the book.)

These twelve pentomino pieces are each made from five cubelets of wenge. To make the appearance more interesting, I try to glue the cubelets so that the grains alternate.

Pen-Ten-Gee (Pentomino Challenge)

I have created a game for two people using two sets of pentominoes of contrasting woods. Each set can be made from 60 cubelets, or, alternatively, with pieces of stick cut to 1, 2, 3, 4, and 5 units in length. That is, if the stick is 1 inch by 1 inch, then pieces will be 1 inch, 2 inches, 3 inches, 4 inches, and 5 inches long. One set of pentominoes requires one 5-unit piece, two 4-unit pieces, five 3-unit pieces, twelve 2-unit pieces, and eight 1-unit pieces. After gluing up both sets, the pieces can be sanded and their edges eased, if desired, with a 1/8-inch round-over bit.

Craft two sets of pentominoes and a game board to play Pen-ten-gee, a challenging game where the most forward-thinking opponent wins.

The game board for Pen-ten-gee consists of a field of 120 squares. It is framed with 3/4-inch or 1-inch square sticks. The inner dimensions of the frame measure 10 cubelets by 12 cubelets. Miter the ends of all the frame sticks to 45 degrees, and cut a 1/4-inch deep slot 1/8 inch up from the bottom. Make the game board from a 1/4-inch thick rectangle of good (birch or oak) plywood cut to a dimension of 10 units plus 3/8 inch of extra space by 12 units plus 3/8 inch of space. Glue up the frame with the plywood set in the grooves. Hold the pieces while the glue dries with a frame clamp—I make a simple frame clamp, as shown on pg. 34, from eight pieces of hardwood, four 18-inch lengths of 1/4-inch threaded rod, eight 1/4-inch nuts, and four 1/4-inch wing nuts or sliding nuts. You can also purchase commercial frame clamps if you wish.

PEN-TEN-GEE

(Pentomino Challenge)

An exciting, thought-provoking, easy-to-learn game of spacial relationships for two players. Ages 8 to adult.

PEN-TEN-GEE consists of two sets of 12 pentominoes and a game board with 120 squares. Each pentomino piece is made up of 5 cubes, arranged in the 12 possible ways that they can be connected in two dimensions.

OBJECT: The object of the game is to play more of your pentominoes on the game board than your opponent. If both players play the same number of pentominoes, the game is a draw.

PLAY: The player who begins places one pentomino so that it covers one or more of the center squares. Then each player in turn places an additional piece on the board. If a player cannot play a piece, he pahe or she passes and the opposing player plays all of the pieces that can legally be played. When placing a pentomino, these rules apply:

1. Each piece (except for the first) must touch a piece already on the board by at least one cube face. A piece cannot just touch corner to corner.

2. As the pieces are played, spaces or holes may be created between the pieces and/or the edges of the game board. Any space must consist of 5 or more adjacent squares (and the squares cannot touch corner to corner). A space may conform to the shape of a pentomino piece, but does not have to.

HINT: Watch which pieces your opponent plays. Try to create a space on the game board that conforms to a played piece. Better yet, create a space to suit one of your pieces so you can play it later.

ADDITIONAL FUN: Pentominoes can be used to create many, many different shapes. Create a shape and then challenge your opponent to copy it.

Storage layout for one set of pentominoes

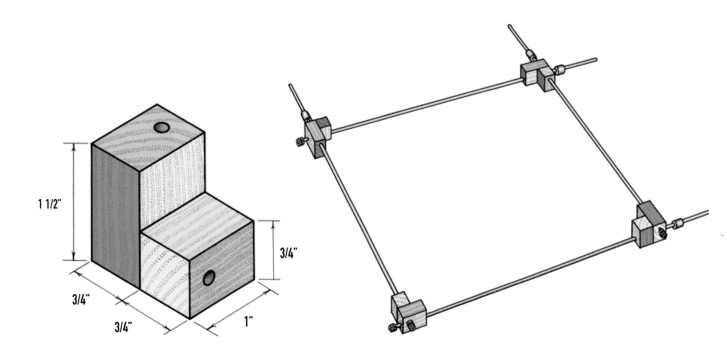

1 1/2"

3/4"

3/4"

3/4"

1"

This is how the frame clamp, a simple but useful tool, goes together.

After the glue has dried, draw the grid on the plywood with a pencil or a permanent fine-tipped marker. I usually print out the directions (on the previous page), and laminate the page to the back of the game board so it won't get lost.

CHAPTER 4

Puzzles from disks

These two lighthouse puzzles are made from disks. At left is a lighthouse ball maze, at right is a "Tower of Quoddy" puzzle.

Low many ways can you think of to make a wooden disk? I can think of several. You can draw a circle and cut it out with a scroll saw, band saw, or fret saw. You could use a dedicated circle cutter (a fixed pivot) on a band saw or table saw. Another option would be to use a single-arm or double-arm circle cutter on a drill press, or a circular template and a router. Don't forget the possibility of using a pivoting attachment on the router or saber saw. Additionally, you could turn a cylinder of wood on a lathe, then slice off disks. Use a plug cutter on the drill press. You could also use a hole saw on the drill press.

Making wooden disks

The easiest way to cut wood disks is with a hole saw on a drill press. Because I cut a lot of disks, I invested in carbide-tipped hole saws of varying sizes. They have offset teeth, which cut a kerf through the wood about 3/32 inch wide. The pilot hole in the center is useful in further machining of the disks. This hole allows the disks to be mounted on a threaded rod for turning with a drill press. It also provides a "holder" hole for some of the jigs shown later. Remember that the hole saw size reflects the size of the hole it will cut—after finishing, the disk is about 1/4 inch less in diameter than the hole saw.

Start the process by attaching a sacrificial board, from which to create a kerfed template, to the drill-press table. Cut into the board with the hole saw to a depth of about 1/16 inch. (Be sure the board is thick enough so the pilot drill won't go all the way through.) Using this cut as a guide, align one or two edges of the wood with the hole so that the edge(s) is in the middle of the template kerf. When you drill, you'll find that sawdust can easily escape because half the thickness of the hole saw extends out of the wood (at top right). Note that with a hole saw having a thin blade, this may not be possible.

Another trick to make disk-cutting more efficient is to finish the cut from the other side. Regardless of the thickness of the wood from which the disk is being cut, set the depth stop so that the cut finishes about 1/16 inch shy of completion. Flip the wood over, complete the cut, and remove the disk from the hole saw.

Sand and finish the disks while turning them on the drill press (at bottom right). It's easy to make a disk holder from a 10-inch long 1/4-inch diameter threaded rod, three 1/4-inch nuts, and a few spacers made from 1/4-inch washers or 5/16-inch nuts. Hold the rod in the drill press chuck; stabilize it at the other end in a 1/4-inch interior-diameter (ID) bushing or bearing set in a board clamped to the drill-press table.

The pencil at the bottom of the photo points at the kerf in the template board. The kerf lets sawdust escape when cutting a disk with a hole saw.

It's easy to sand a stack of disks on the drill press using a homemade holder made from threaded rod.

This elegant puzzle is both fun to play with and look at. Dead-end passages in each level makes finding the solution to this puzzle a challenge. Woods included in this puzzle are padauk, zebrawood, wenge, and cherry.

Lighthouse Ball Maze

This "route-finding" or "sequential-movement" puzzle is based on an ancient puzzle called "The Pagoda." The object of the puzzle is to place a ball in the top of the lighthouse, move it from layer to layer by twisting the sections of the lighthouse, and have it exit through a hole in the base. In each layer of the lighthouse, however, there are dead ends, making this puzzle tricky to solve.

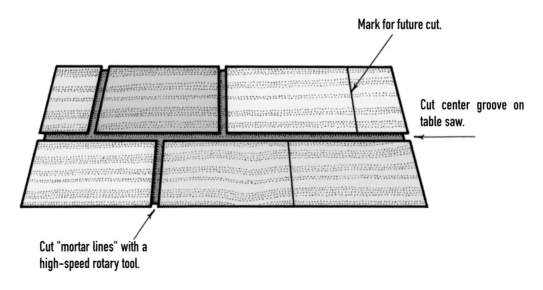

Mark for future cut.

Cut center groove on table saw.

Cut "mortar lines" with a high-speed rotary tool.

The lighthouse-puzzle base is made from a piece of 1-1/4-inch thick wood. The cuts make it resemble brick or stonework.

Make the base of the lighthouse from a 1-1/4 thick piece of wood such as black walnut, or, in this case, padauk. Cut it 3-3/4 inches square and bevel all sides at 25 degrees. Saw a 1/8-inch deep groove across the middle of each beveled side, then cut vertical grooves with a high-speed rotary tool to imitate brick or stonework. Drill a 1/4-inch hole in the center of the top to a depth of 3/4 inch.

The body of the lighthouse is made from seven disks of 3/4-inch wood. Alternating disks cut of wood of two contrasting colors, such as padauk and maple, or black walnut and ash, or, in this case, wenge and zebrawood, give the lighthouse a nice appearance. The upper edges of the bottom three disks, cut with 2-3/4-inch, 2-1/2-inch, and 2-1/4-inch hole saws, are shaped with a 1/4-inch rounding-over bit. The upper four disks, each cut with a 2-inch hole saw, have slightly eased edges.

The top of the lighthouse is made from three pieces of wood selected for their contrasting colors. To make the walkway, which is the lowest layer of the lighthouse top, drill a 1-7/8-inch diameter hole 1/8 inch deep into the wood. Using the center of the hole as a guide, cut out the disk containing this hole with a 2-1/4-inch hole saw. The bottom edge of the walkway can be shaped by turning on a vertical lathe (pg. 42).

Make the light from a piece of light-colored wood (1-3/4 inches by 1-3/4 inches by 1-1/4 inches). Bevel the sides to reduce each of them to 1 inch wide. In the middle of each of the four original sides, drill a 3/4-inch hole 1/8 inch deep. Glue a padauk plug in each hole, then sand the plugs flush. Through the center of one of the plugs and into the cube, drill a 1/2-inch hole to a total depth of 5/8 inch. A 1/4-inch hole is then drilled through the center of the block, top to bottom.

The roof is made from a disk cut with a 2-1/4-inch hole saw from a 1-inch piece of contrasting wood. Just as with the walkway, a 1-7/8-inch hole that is 1/8 inch deep is first drilled in the wood. The center hole is drilled and the disk is contoured to the desired shape by turning on the vertical lathe.

The three parts of the lighthouse top

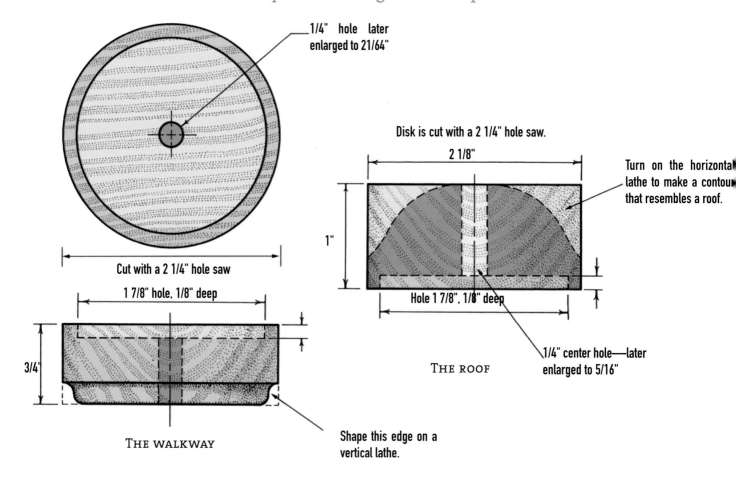

1/4" hole later enlarged to 21/64"

Disk is cut with a 2 1/4" hole saw.

2 1/8"

1"

Turn on the horizontal lathe to make a contour that resembles a roof.

Hole 1 7/8", 1/8" deep

THE ROOF

1/4" center hole—later enlarged to 5/16"

Cut with a 2 1/4" hole saw

1 7/8" hole, 1/8" deep

3/4"

THE WALKWAY

Shape this edge on a vertical lathe.

THE LIGHT

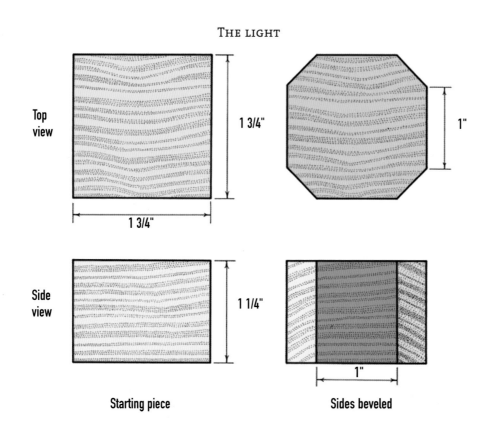

Top view

1 3/4"

1 3/4"

1"

Side view

1 1/4"

1"

Starting piece

Sides beveled

DRILLING THE HOLES IN THE LIGHT

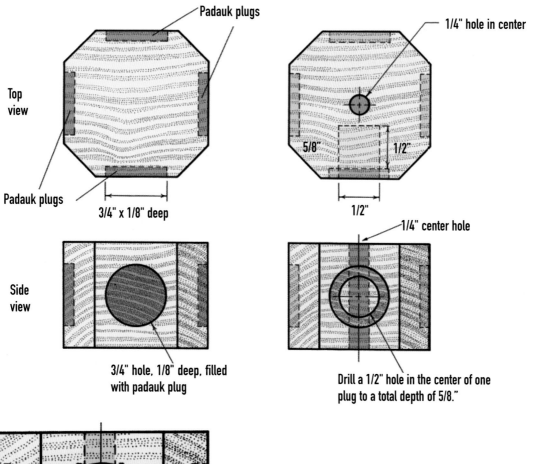

Top view — Padauk plugs · Padauk plugs · 3/4" x 1/8" deep

1/4" hole in center · 5/8" · 1/2" · 1/2"

Side view — 3/4" hole, 1/8" deep, filled with padauk plug

1/4" center hole

Drill a 1/2" hole in the center of one plug to a total depth of 5/8."

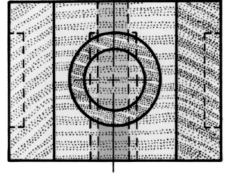

Side view

The bottom of the light

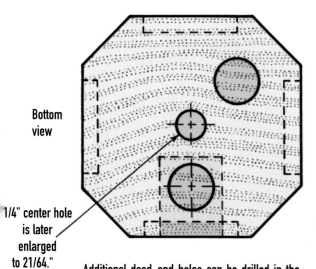

Bottom view

1/4" center hole is later enlarged to 21/64."

Additional dead-end holes can be drilled in the bottom using a jig (pg. 43)—each hole is 1" deep.

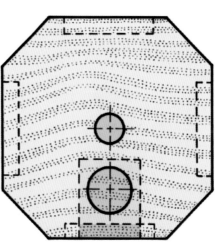

A 13/32" hole 1" deep, is drilled later using the jig described (pg. 43). This hole must intersect the 1/2" hole in the side of the piece.

Now that the pieces are made, it's time to create the maze. I like to use a 3/8-inch steel ball for this puzzle, so the maze holes should be 7/16 inch and later slightly enlarged at each end with a countersink bit. All the holes in all the pieces must be at a uniform distance from the center hole of each piece. This is done by making a simple jig as follows: In a board on the drill-press table, drill a 1/4-inch hole and place in it a 1/4-inch dowel so that 1/2 inch of dowel protrudes from the hole. Place a 7/16-inch bit in the chuck.

A Vertical Lathe for the Drill Press

In the center of a 3-inch by 12-inch piece of hardwood that's 1 inch thick (maple and oak are good), drill a 1/2-inch or 5/8-inch hole, depending on the OD of the bushing or bearing that you choose. The depth of this hole should be sufficient to allow the bushing/bearing to sit flush with the surface of the wood. Drill a 1-inch hole 2-1/2 inches from the center of the bearing, and glue in a 10-inch long piece of 1-inch dowel. Clamp the board to the drill-press table with the bearing centered under the chuck. Mount the disks to be shaped on a length of 1/4-inch threaded rod; the dowel acts as the tool rest. If needed, the rod can be strengthened with sections of hollow 3/8-inch rod (typically used in lamps).

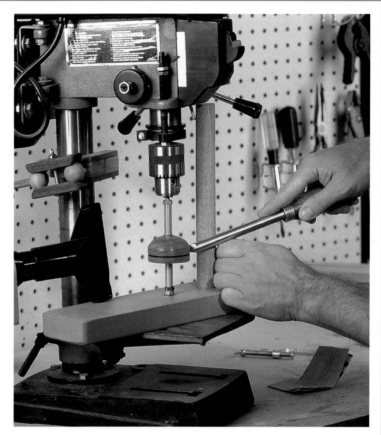

The lighthouse roof is efficiently shaped on the vertical lathe. The chisel is held steady against a dowel tool rest.

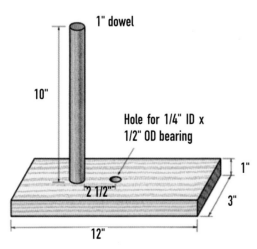

1" dowel

10"

Hole for 1/4" ID x 1/2" OD bearing

1"

2 1/2"

3"

12"

A vertical lathe for the drill press is simple to make and saves lots of time in the shaping process.

Create dead ends by drilling multiple holes in each disk of the lighthouse body. The disks are held on a jig consisting of a dowel that protrudes from a piece of plywood. This jig helps ensure that the through hole and the dead-end holes are equidistant from the center hole.

Move and reclamp the jig so that the bit is centered 3/8 inch from the edge of the dowel. Machine each of the pieces except the roof, base, and light by placing one on the dowel and drilling one hole all the way through. Then rotate the piece and drill additional holes, each only 1/2 inch deep, in the top and/or bottom of each disk. The greater the number of dead-end holes, the tougher the puzzle will be to solve.

Place the light on the dowel and position it to drill a hole that's 1 inch deep in the bottom and intersects the 1/2-hole already in the block. (See the bottom of the drawing on pg.41.) Additional dead-end holes can be drilled in the bottom of this piece as well.

Drill the lighthouse base while holding it at a 5-degree angle. This will let you create a sloped exit hole.

Now drill the exit hole in the base. Place a 1/4-inch dowel in the base's center hole, then place the largest disk on the dowel. Rotate the disk so that the through hole is centered on one of the base's beveled sides. Use the through hole as a guide to drill a 7/16-inch hole only 1/8 inch deep in the top of the base to mark its location. The base is then repositioned so that a 1/2-inch hole can be drilled from the beveled side to run directly under the 7/16-inch hole. This 1/2-inch hole will be about 1-1/2 inches deep. This hole should provide a slight downward slope when the base sits flat, to allow the steel ball to roll out of the base. It helps to hold the base in a drill-press angle vise set at 5 degrees. Next, the 7/16-inch hole is deepened so that it intersects the 1/2-inch hole. Drop a ball bearing in this hole to make sure it will roll out of the base.

Next, slightly enlarge the openings of each of the 7/16-inch holes, the hole in the base, the holes in the seven disks, the walkway, and the light with a countersink. Enlarging the holes will help compensate for any moisture-related movement of the pieces. Inspect all the pieces to make sure the holes are free of debris. Next, enlarge the center hole in the base to 5/16 inch to a depth of 3/4 inch. Enlarge the center hole in the roof to 5/16 inch all the way through. Enlarge the center holes in the seven disks, the walkway, and the light to 21/64 inch all the way through.

Glue an 11-inch length of 5/16-inch hardwood dowel into the center hole of the base and round the other end. Place the lighthouse pieces—in order—on the dowel. Before you glue on the roof, which holds all the pieces together, run a ball through the maze to ensure that there aren't any hang-ups. If the ball moves freely, remove the pieces, give them their final finish, and put them back in place. Glue the roof to the dowel, being careful that no glue squeezes out onto the piece below, and that the pieces between base and roof all turn freely. The puzzle is ready for use.

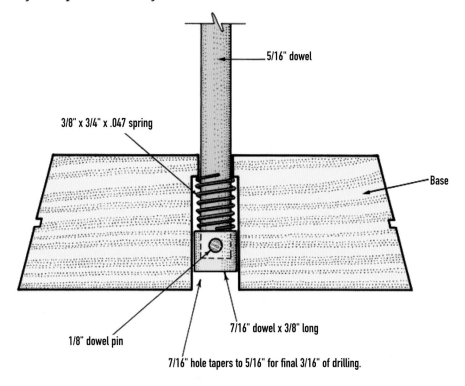

Use this modified construction if you're concerned about excessive swings in humidity, which can cause a puzzle to stop working well.

I have found that this puzzle can be affected adversely by humidity changes, especially if the disks are cut from quartersawn wood. (Think about the grain orientation.) I have added a modification to this puzzle to compensate for dimensional changes. Everything about the puzzle is the same except:

The base is drilled differently. A 7/16-inch hole is drilled in the bottom, stopping 3/16 inch short of penetration. This hole is reduced to 5/16 inch for the final 3/16 inch. A 5/16-inch dowel should be snug in this hole but move with slight effort.

The center dowel is modified. A 3/8-inch length of 7/16-inch dowel has a 5/16-inch hole drilled in its center lengthwise to a depth of 1/4 inch. This machined piece is glued on the end of a 12-inch length of 5/16-inch dowel. For increased strength, a 1/8-inch dowel pins the pieces together. Sand the ends of the dowel pin flush. Sand this piece of 7/16-inch dowel lightly so that it is snug but moves with little effort in the hole.

A 3/4-inch length of 3/8-inch .047 spring is placed on the bottom of the dowel before the dowel is placed in the base. The lighthouse is assembled up to the roof, the dowel assembly is pushed in, the amount determined by the humidity at the time the puzzle is made. In humid conditions, such as in the northeast in summertime, push the spring to full compression and allow the dowel to back out about 1/8 inch. In dry conditions, that is, winter, allow the dowel to back out about 3/8 inch. This will allow room for the disks to swell in moister times. The upper end of the dowel is cut, tapered, rounded, and sanded to its final length of 3/4 inch above the roof.

"Tower of Quoddy"

The lighthouse at West Quoddy, Maine, was originally commissioned by Thomas Jefferson. Its beacon shines from the easternmost locale in the U.S. This puzzle, a sequential-movement puzzle, is my American version of an ancient puzzle called by various names including "Pyramid" and "Tower of Hanoi." The concept of the puzzle is simplicity itself—there are three posts and seven pieces of decreasing diameter that form a lighthouse. The object is to move the lighthouse from one post to another. One piece is moved at a time, and a piece never can sit on a piece smaller in diameter than itself.

While the concept of this puzzle is simple, its successful completion takes a minimum of 127 moves. This can be calculated as follows: the number of moves equals two to the n th power minus 1, where n equals the number of puzzle pieces to be moved.

Done perfectly, this takes 127 moves. The puzzle is easy to make and, when attractive hardwoods are used, the final product is beautiful.

Make the body from six disks. I like to use alternating pieces of padauk or bloodwood and ash or maple (the Quoddy lighthouse has red and white horizontal stripes). Cut the disks with the following hole saws: 3-1/4 inch, 3 inch, 2-3/4 inch, 2-1/2 inch, 2-1/4 inch, and 2-inch. Shape the top edge of each disk with a 1/4-inch round-over bit.

Make the light from a piece of 1-1/2-inch by 1-1/2-inch by 1-1/4-inch light-colored wood. Bevel each side so the final width of each side is 1 inch. The final shape will resemble an octagon. On each of the four original sides, drill a 1/2-inch hole that's 1/8 inch deep and insert padauk plugs. Drill a 9/16-inch hole through its center top to bottom.

Construct the lighthouse roof from a 3/4-inch thick, 1-5/8-inch disk of dark-colored wood. Shape it into a roof on the vertical lathe (pg. 42). The walkway is made from a 1-5/8-inch disk that's 3/8-inch thick, rounded over at the bottom. Each of the circular pieces can be sanded and finished by turning on the drill press. Then enlarge the center hole in each of the pieces to 9/16 inch. Glue the walkway, light, and roof together to make one piece.

The puzzle base consists of a piece of 4-1/4-inch by 10-1/2-inch by 3/4-inch hardwood. Bevel the edges of the piece at 25 degrees. Cut a 1/8-inch horizontal groove in the middle of each beveled side with the table saw. Use a high-speed rotary tool to cut vertical grooves that simulate brickwork. Drill three 1/2-inch holes for the posts—one in the center and the other two 3-1/4 inches away, center-to-center, each to a depth of 1/2 inch. Insert three 8-1/4-inch lengths of 1/2-inch dowel in these holes after the top ends have been sanded to a rounded point.

CHAPTER 5

Puzzles from rings

Many wonderful mazes may be made from rings, dowels, and rope. Shown here are both vertical and horizontal ring-and-rope maze puzzles. "Triple Bogey" (center), is a fun puzzle with a golf theme.

I̲t's easy to make a ring from a disk by enlarging the hole left by the hole saw. The rings most appropriate for the puzzles shown here are about 2 inches in diameter (cut with a 2-1/4-inch hole saw), with a 1-1/4-inch hole cut in the center. Start with a sanded, finished disk having both edges shaped with a 1/4-inch round-over router bit.

Here's how to center the hole: Clamp a board on the drill-press table and drill a 1/4-inch hole about 1/2-inch deep. In this hole place a 3/4-inch long piece of 1/4-inch dowel. Put the disk on the dowel and, while holding it securely with the disk-holder shown below and on the next page, drill a 1-1/4-inch hole to a depth of about 1/8 inch. Turn over the disk and drill a hole 3/8 inch deep. Then remove the disk, remove the dowel, and finish drilling the hole. The edges of the hole can be eased slightly or rounded over with a 1/8-inch or 1/4-inch round-over bit. For safety while routing, attach the ring with double-stick tape to a larger piece of wood.

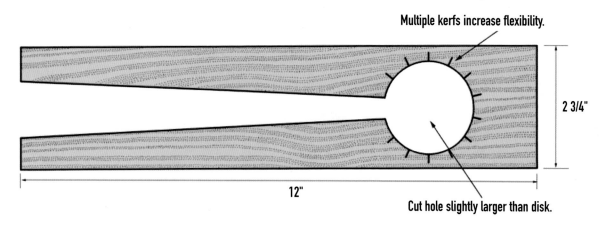

Multiple kerfs increase flexibility.

2 3/4"

12"

Cut hole slightly larger than disk.

This handy disk holder is made from 3/4-inch softwood. It makes drilling disks easy and safe.

For most of my puzzles, I attach the rings to 3/8-inch dowels. I made a jig, which you may find helpful, to help drill dowel holes in the center of the side of a ring and perpendicular to it (next page, bottom right). To make the jig, drill a hole slightly larger than the ring in a 4-inch by 3-inch by 3/4-inch piece of wood, with the lower extent of the hole 1/4-inch from the bottom edge and in the midline. Drill a 3/8-inch hole in the center of the top of the jig. Attach a piece of wood over the large hole on one side as a backer board to help hold the ring in position for drilling.

A disk-holding jig grasps the disk securely, keeping your guide hand well removed from the bit and ensuring an accurate cut.

This dowel-hole-drilling jig helps you cut a hole in the center of the ring side and perpendicular to it.

Vertical Ring and Rope Maze Puzzle

I have given these original "tanglement" puzzles various names depending on their themes. The theme is defined by the object in the center of the puzzle and the object on the rope that is to be removed. For example, in the "Unchain My Heart" puzzle, the center object is a heart, and there is a black ball on a black rope (or fine chain, for increased difficulty). In "Strike Three," the center object is a baseball and the object on the rope is a baseball bat. In "Par 6" I use a real golf ball in the center, and a golf club on the rope. And in "Lost in Space," the puzzle featured here, the center object is a moon and the object on the rope is a star.

In "Lost in Space," as in all tanglement puzzles, the object is to free the rope from the rings. Solving requires a number of repetitive steps.

It's probably easier to create this puzzle than to solve it. Start by making four rings as described previously. To make the frame, assemble four 7-3/8-inch long 3/4-inch square sticks using miter joints. Drill a 3/8-inch hole that is 1/2-inch deep on the shorter face of each stick—locate it 1-3/8 inches from the miter. On one stick, drill an additional hole at the center (next page, top right).

Glue the sticks into a square (next page, bottom right). Use a frame clamp to hold the sticks while the glue dries. When the glue is dry, strengthen each joint by inserting a 3/8-inch dowel or a feather spline across each joint.

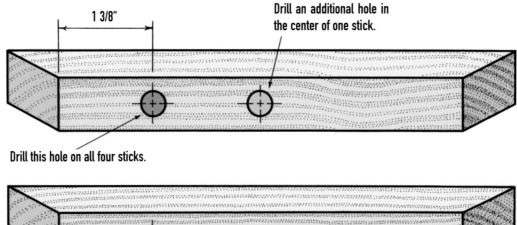

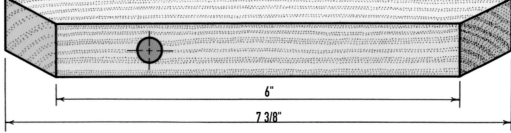

1 3/8"

Drill an additional hole in the center of one stick.

Drill this hole on all four sticks.

6"

7 3/8"

Four mitered sticks form the frame of the vertical ring and rope puzzle.

Orient the frame pieces so the holes fall as they are shown here.

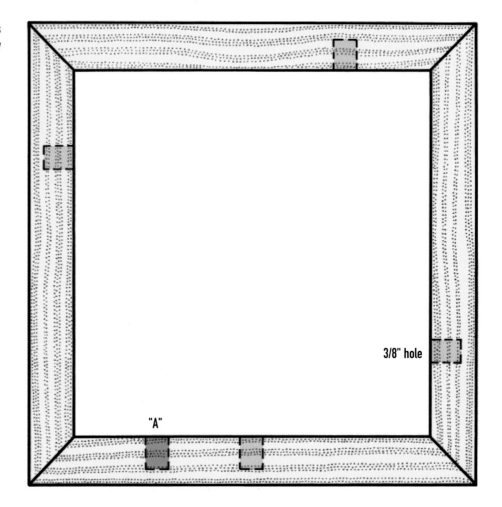

3/8" hole

"A"

Make the moon from two pieces of 1/2-inch thick stock, one a light wood, one dark. Cut the wood into 2-inch disks without center holes. (I use a large plug cutter or remove the pilot drill from the hole saw.) Stack the disks with double-stick tape between, draw a half-moon, and cut through both disks with a scroll saw. Separate the pieces, glue together a light moon and dark background, and drill a 3/8-inch hole 3/8-inch deep into the disk bottom. Sand the disk smooth and ease the edges.

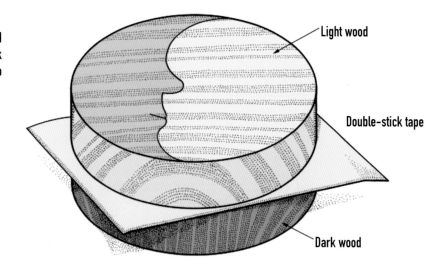

The moon disks are held together with double-stick tape for scroll-sawing into half-moon shapes.

Light wood

Double-stick tape

Dark wood

Cut a star out of 1/2-inch or 3/4-inch thick wood—make it about 2 inches across. Drill a 3/16-inch hole from the tip of one arm straight through to the opposite crotch. Enlarge the hole to 3/8 inch for a depth of 1 inch at the crotch. Ease or round over the edges. Next, cut five lengths of 3/8-inch hardwood dowel, three at 4-1/2 inches, one at 2-3/4 inches, and one at 2-7/8 inches. Taper each end slightly. Glue the first four dowels into the rings and the fifth into the moon. Glue the dowels in order into the frame, starting with the one in the hole labeled "A" in the frame drawing on the previous page and moving

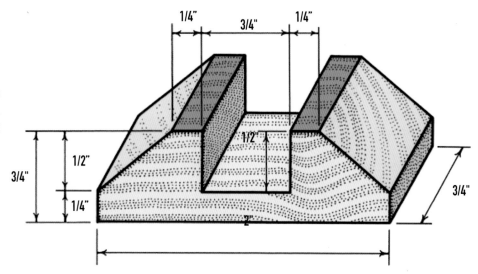

Cut two feet to attach to the bottom of the frame, to hold the puzzle in a vertical position.

1/4" 3/4" 1/4"

1/2"

3/4"

1/2"

1/4"

3/4"

clockwise. You might have to trim the dowels slightly to fit. Finally, cut out two feet and glue them to the bottom of the frame. Use wood that matches the frame so the puzzle will look nice.

Use a 25-inch length of soft, 1/8-inch-diameter cord for the rope. Knot the ends together. Pull the loop through the hole in the star from larger diameter to smaller, pulling the knotted ends snugly into the star. Glue a 3/8-inch plug behind the knot, trim it flush, and finish the star. Apply finish to the puzzle, let it dry, then maneuver the cord onto the puzzle in reverse order of its solution.

Placing the cord on "Lost in Space" (Solution is the reverse)

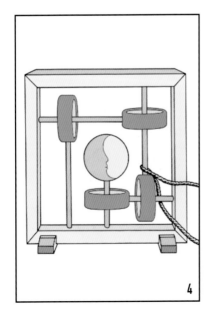

1

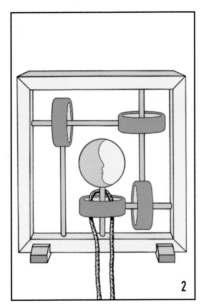

2

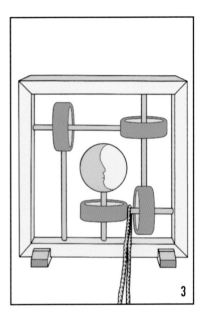

3

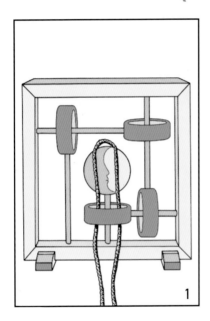

4

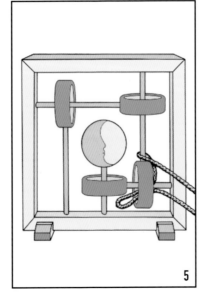

5

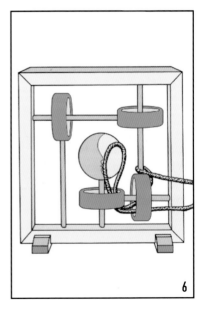

6

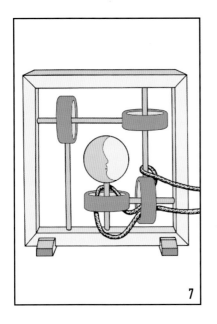

7

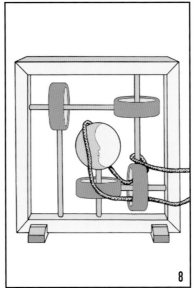

8

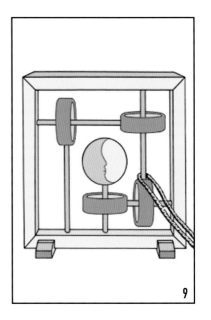

9

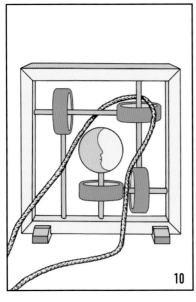

10

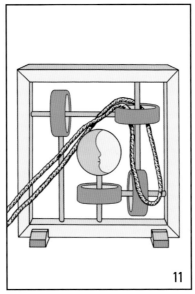

11

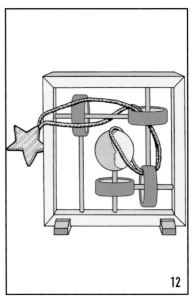

12

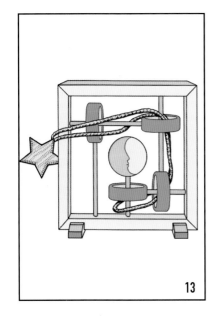

13

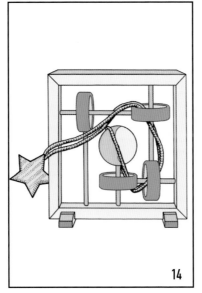

14

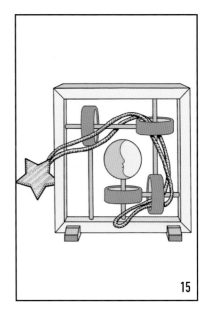

15

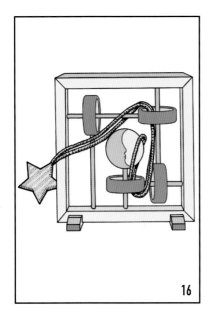

16

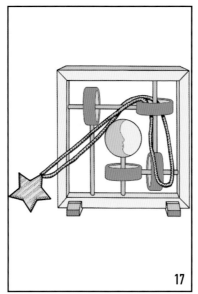

17

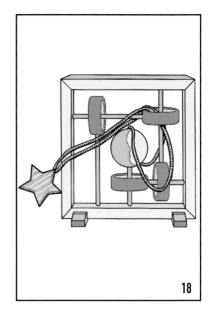

18

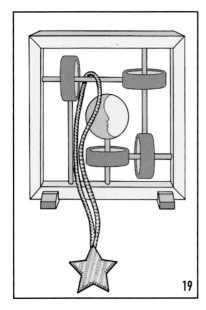

19

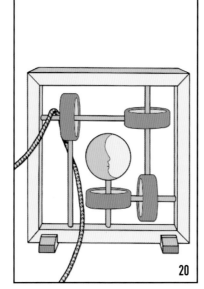

20

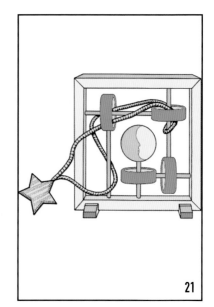

21

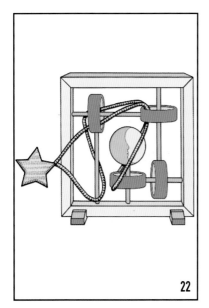

22

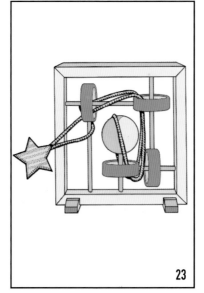

23

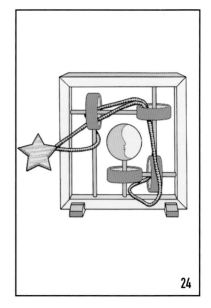

24

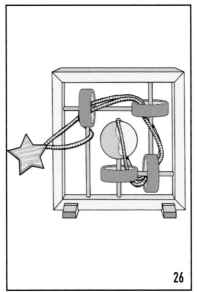

25

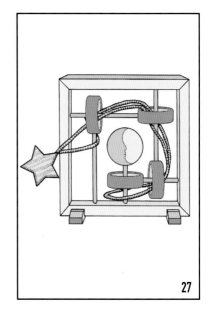

26

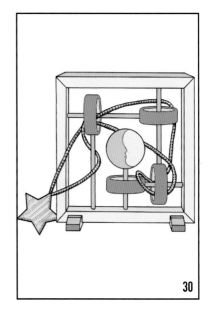

27

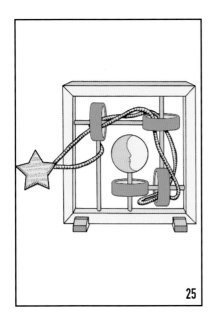

28

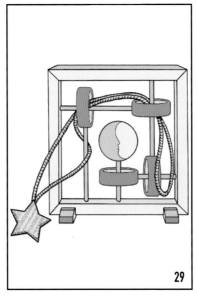

29

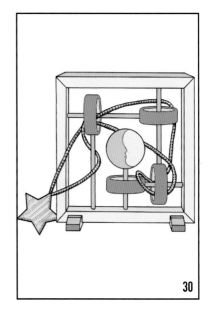

30

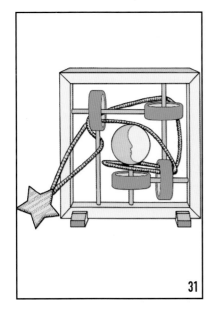

31

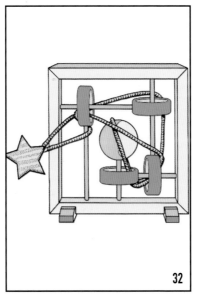

32

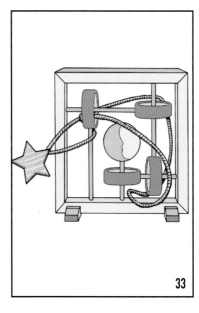

33

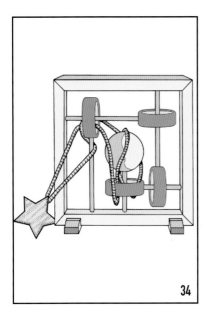

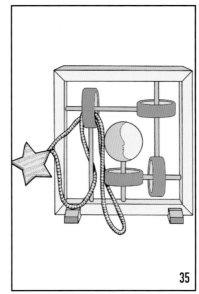

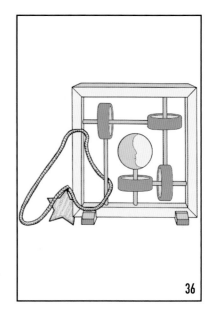

34

35

36

Horizontal Ring and Rope Maze Puzzle

I have created two puzzles of this type, one with a baseball theme called "Home Run," and one with a golf theme called "Triple Bogey." In "Home Run," the base is shaped like home plate, the center object is a baseball, and the object on the rope is a baseball bat. The base of "Triple Bogey" is shaped to model a putting green, the center object is a golf ball, and the rope attaches to a golf club.

The thematic motifs used in vertical ring and rope maze puzzles work just as well in the horizontal mode. "Triple Bogey" features a real golf ball and a wooden putter.

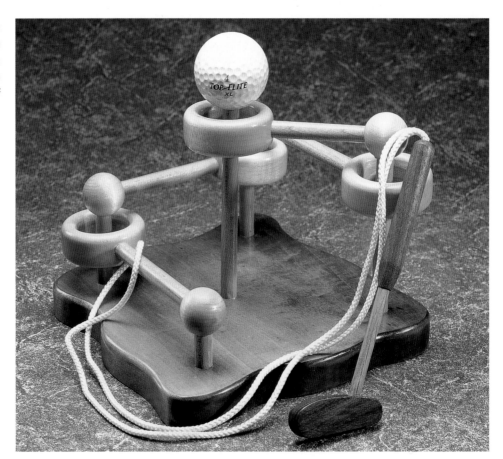

Begin construction of this puzzle by making four rings as previously described. Then make the base. Use 3/4-inch stock that measures roughly 7-1/2 inches square. After cutting the curved shape, ease the edges and dye the wood green with water-based aniline dye. Drill five 3/8-inch holes in the base to a depth of 1/2 inch—one in the center and four around the periphery.

Each ring is held by two lengths of 3/8-inch dowel—a vertical piece and a horizontal piece joined by a 3/4-inch ball. Each of the four wooden balls has two 3/8-inch holes drilled 3/8 inch deep and 90 degrees apart. Here's how I drill the holes in the balls: Drill a 1/2-inch hole 1/2 inch deep into a board clamped on the drill-press table. Without changing any other settings, place a ball in the hole and change the bit to 3/8 inch. Drill the first hole, and insert a 4-inch length of 3/8-inch dowel. Put the ball back in the hole and hold the dowel parallel to the table with the help of a spacer to drill the second hole (below). Using this technique, the second hole will be perpendicular to the first one.

A hole in a board clamped to the drill-press table holds the wood ball securely for accurate drilling. A spacer under the dowel keeps the second hole absolutely perpendicular to the first hole.

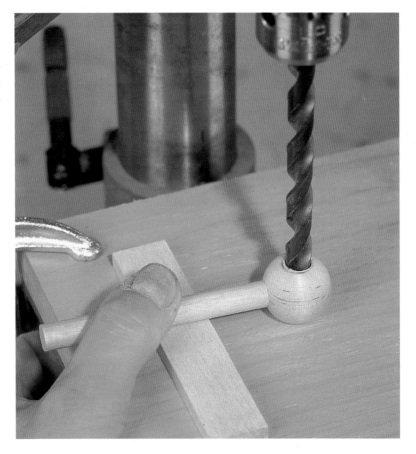

Cut the five vertical dowel pieces to 1-3/4 inch, 2-3/4 inch, 3-3/4 inch, 4-3/4 inch, and 5-3/4 inch long; slightly taper both ends. Glue the dowels in the holes in the base. Custom-cut the five horizontal dowels to length, determined by the distance between the two holes each will span. For each dowel, measure from hole center to hole center, then subtract roughly 5/8 inch. Dry-fit each dowel and trim as necessary so that each ring is centered on the next vertical dowel. Taper the dowel end slightly and glue a ball on one end. Glue each ball on its vertical dowel, then glue a ring on the end of the horizontal dowel. Drill a 3/8-inch hole 1/2 inch deep in a golf ball, and glue the ball on the center dowel with cyanoacrylate or epoxy because regular wood glue doesn't hold this material well. After applying a coat of finish to this part of the puzzle, you can then spread small areas of glue on the "green" with a brush and sprinkle on green-stained wood chips for the appearance of grass.

The golf club handle is made from a 3-inch length of 1/2-inch dowel, and the shaft from a 4-inch length of 1/4-inch dowel. The head is cut from a 1/2-inch thick piece of wood measuring 3/4 inch by 2 inches. To begin, drill a 3/16-inch hole lengthwise through the center of the 1/2-inch dowel; enlarge the hole to 1/4 inch for 2-1/2 inches of its length. Round the end of the dowel with the narrower hole and taper the other end. Knot each end of a 36-inch length of 1/8-inch-diameter cord and hold them together to form a loop. Pass the loop through the larger handle hole and out through the smaller hole, pulling the knots taut into the handle. Glue the shaft into the handle. Cut out the head of the putter using a scroll saw. The shaft is glued to the putter head in a 3/8-inch deep, 1/4-inch-diameter hole drilled in the putter at a slight angle to perpendicular. After finishing the golf club, maneuver the cord onto the puzzle. This is not shown, since I've deliberately left it for you to figure out. This is a puzzle book, after all. But here's a hint: the solution is similar to the one given for the vertical ring and rope maze puzzle.

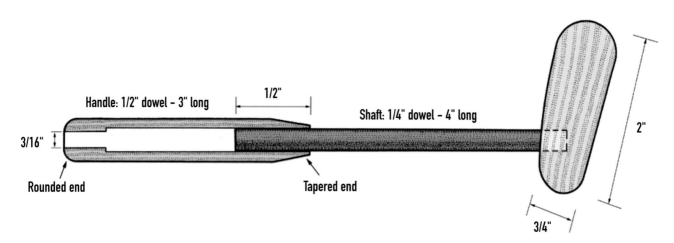

Before assembling the shaft and handle, insert the puzzle cord from the wider end of the handle and pull it through the narrower end—the knotted ends will stop its travel.

"I'm Your Handyman"

The name of this puzzle comes from the song of the same name, which includes the phrase "if your broken heart's in need of repair..." The object of the puzzle is to put two parts of a broken heart back together.

Tanglement puzzles may be made in many shapes. The puzzles shown above don't have rings like the others in this chapter, but instead use full-size wooden tools. They're based on an ancient African rope puzzle, and great to give as presents. Construction isn't difficult. Just cut the shape on a scroll saw, round over the edges with a router, and drill a few holes. All four puzzles are made the same way.

Start with a 5-inch by 2-1/2-inch rectangle of 3/4-inch thick wood. I like black walnut and oak for these puzzles. Copy the outline of the puzzle onto the wood, and cut it out on the scroll saw. Round over the edges with a 1/8-inch round-over bit. Drill a 1/2-inch hole through the tool shape face, then two 5/32-inch holes in the bottom edge, each to a depth of 3/8 inch.

Cut the heart from a 2-inch square of 3/4-inch padauk or blood-wood. Drill a 1/4-inch hole through the heart, bevel the edges of the hole, and round over the edges with a 1/8-inch bit. Cut the heart in half with a jagged line. Sand and finish the wooden parts. Loop an 18-inch length of 1/8-inch-diameter cord through the puzzle and through the heart halves, and glue each end into one of the holes in the tool shape with gel cyanoacrylate glue, which works well for this puzzle.

61

Full size tool templates

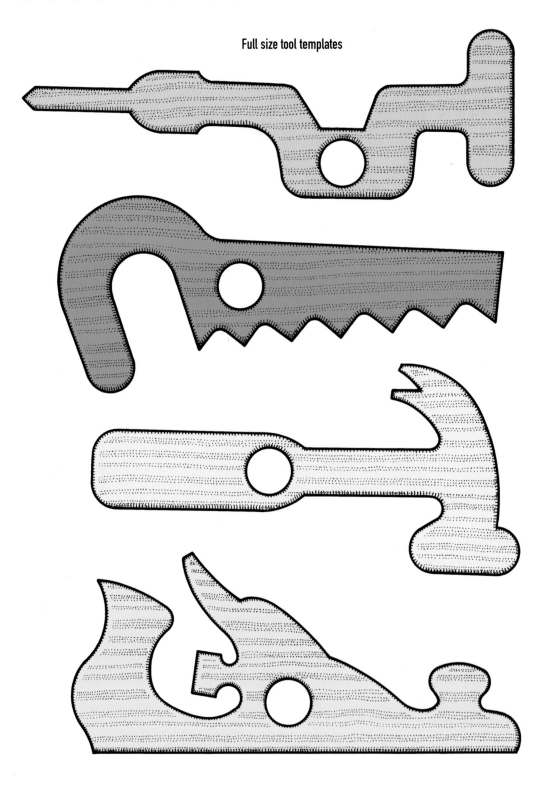

Full size tool templates

Solution for "I'm Your Handyman"

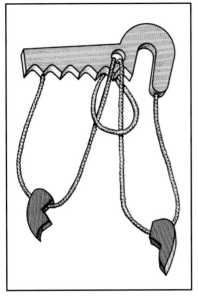
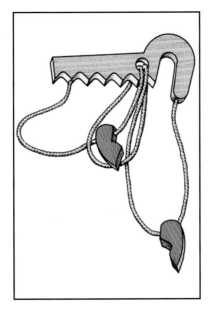
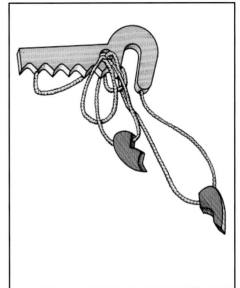
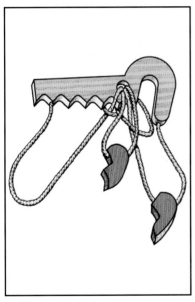
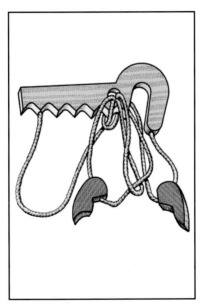
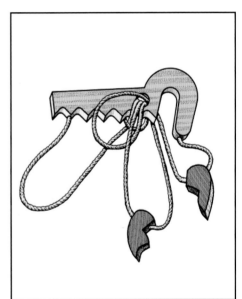
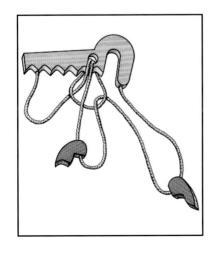
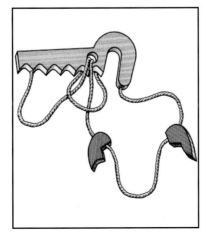
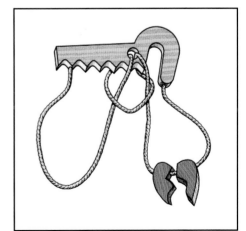

CHAPTER 6

Opening Puzzles

These four handsome puzzles all feature locking mechanisms including such devices as metal pins, magnets, and springs. At top left is a hexagonal dovetail puzzle, at top right is "The Bolt (To Drive You Nuts!)," at lower left is "Heart and ?," and at lower right is "Holy Cross Padlock."

Dalgety and Hordern, a couple of serious puzzle enthusiasts, have developed a system of puzzle classification that groups puzzles into fourteen main classes. To quote from their web site, www.Puzzlemuseum.com, " 'Opening puzzles' are puzzles in which the principle object is to open it, undo it, remove something from it, or otherwise get it to work. They usually comprise a single object or associated parts, such as a box and its lid... The mechanism of the puzzle is not usually apparent..."

Jerry Slocum's puzzle (top) has a center pin held by two horizontal pins. The bottom puzzle incorporates a magnet to hold the center pin.

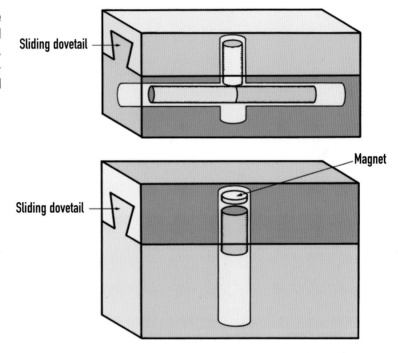

Sliding dovetail

Sliding dovetail

Magnet

This type of wooden puzzle is probably my favorite. It consists of two components: the wooden part—two or more pieces of wood machined into various shapes—and a locking mechanism.

Slocum's two puzzles—In his book, *Puzzles Old and New*, Jerry Slocum depicts two "take-apart" puzzles with simple, elegant locking mechanisms of his own design. The puzzles consist of two rectangular pieces of wood interlocked with a sliding dovetail; in both there is a vertical pin that keeps the pieces from sliding apart. In the first puzzle, the vertical pin can retract only when the two horizontal pins beneath it are separated by centrifugal force, produced by spinning the puzzle. In the second puzzle, the pin is held in place by a magnet until a rap on the puzzle allows the pin to retract. The satisfaction I received from making these puzzles encouraged me to create puzzles of different shapes with a variety of locking mechanisms.

"Holy Cross," or "Grasshoppa" Padlock

(Because I didn't go to Yale and I haven't practiced enough to be a Master... Get it?)

The "Holy Cross" padlock is fairly complex to construct because of the number of processes you must complete to create the locking mechanism. However, no operation by itself is particularly difficult.

This x-ray of the padlock puzzle prototype was taken without the magnet in place.

This cute puzzle makes good use of two of the concepts demonstrated by Slocum's "take-apart" puzzles. Its locking mechanism consists of metal pins that must be freed from a magnet and separated by centrifugal force. You can see an x-ray of my prototype (before I added the magnet) above.

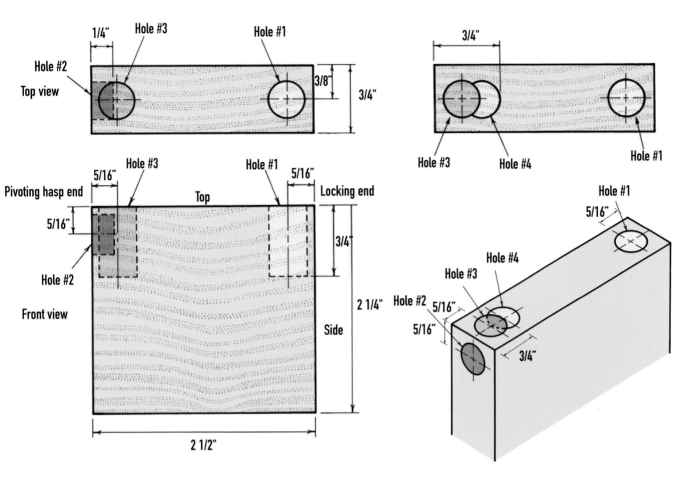

Hole #1 is 7/16" in diameter and 3/4" deep.
Hole center is 5/16" from side.

Hole #3 is 7/16" in diameter and 3/4" deep.
Hole center is 5/16" from side.

Hole #2 is 7/16" in diameter and 1/4" deep.
Hole center is 5/16" from top.

Hole #4 is an extension of hole #3, 3/4" deep.
Edge of hole is 3/4" from edge of the piece.

The locations of the recess for the pivoting part of the hasp and the hole for the locking end are shown here.

To build this puzzle, start with a block of 3/4-inch thick wood measuring 2-1/2 inches wide by 2-1/4 inches tall. This is for the padlock body. I use Brazilian rosewood, bloodwood, or other wood with interesting color or grain.

Drill a 3/4-inch deep, 7/16-inch-diameter hole in the midline of the top (hole #1); set it back 5/16 inch from the edge. At the opposite corner, machine a recess for the pivoting end of the hasp (hole #2): Drill a 7/16-inch hole 1/4 inch deep on the midline of the side, centered 5/16 inch from the top. Drill a 7/16-inch hole 3/4-inch deep in the midline of the top, centered 5/16 inch from the side (hole #3). Enlarge this recess so it extends to 3/4 inch from the edge by drilling an additional hole with a Forstner bit to a depth of 3/4 inch (hole #4). Flatten the sides of the recess with a chisel.

Here's the padlock body and the hasp blank. After cutting, most of the hasp is rounded.

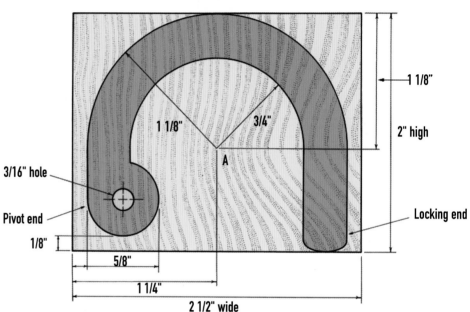

The hasp is cut from a piece of wood 3/8 inch thick. Point A is the midpoint of the width.

Make a hasp from 3/8-inch-thick wood measuring 2-1/2 inches wide by 2 inches high. I prefer mahogany because it shapes easily. The hasp is shaped as shown above. Most of it is sanded round to a diameter of 3/8 inch; the pivoting part is about 5/8 inch wide. The exact location of the hasp ends are marked on the rectangle when it is placed next to the lock body. Note that the pivoting end of the hasp is 1/8 inch shorter than the locking end. Draw the outer curve, roughly a 1-1/8-inch radius, and an inner curve, roughly a 3/4-inch radius, and cut the wood with a scroll saw. Start the process of rounding with a 1/8-inch round-over bit on the router table, but know that you will have to complete most of the rounding by hand-sanding. Slightly taper the inner and outer surfaces of the locking end of the hasp.

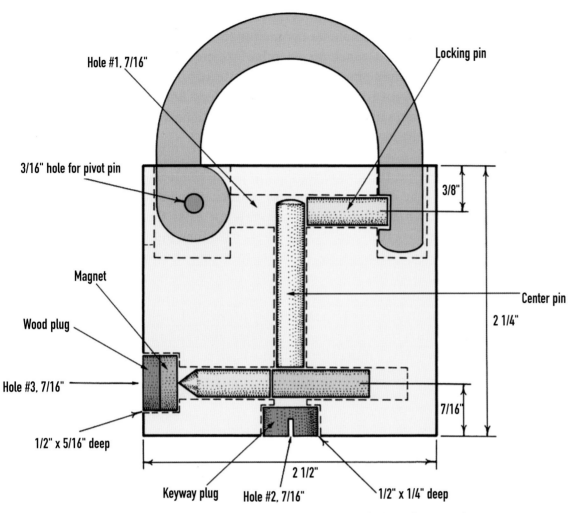

Four metal pins comprise the locking mechanism. The top pin locks the hasp, the center pin prevents the top pin from retracting, and the two bottom pins prevent the center pin from falling. The two bottom pins are kept from sliding by a magnet.

Drill a 3/16-inch hole in the center of the pivoting end, then lay the hasp on the body of the padlock approximating the position it will occupy when locked, and mark the location of the pivot hole. Drill a 3/16-inch pivot hole in the lock body. Place the hasp in the lock body, aligning the pivot hole, and put in a temporary pivot pin. Check the movement. If the hasp doesn't pivot freely, locate where it binds and either sand down the hasp to fit or enlarge the recess in the lock body. When the hasp moves freely, remove the temporary pin and set the hasp aside.

Drill the holes in the lock body for the locking mechanism, which consists of four pins. Cut the bottom pins from 1/4-inch steel rod. You can use 1/4-inch steel or brass rod for the other pins. Drill a 17/64-inch hole for the top pin starting in the recess for the hasp pivot, in the midline, and centered 3/8 inch from the top edge (hole #1). This hole should end in the other hole in the top, the hole for the locking end of the hasp, and not extend through the other side. Drill the 17/64-

inch hole for the center pin from the middle of the bottom of the body until it intersects the hole for the top pin (hole #2). Enlarge the opening of this hole to 1/2 inch for a depth of 1/4 inch. Drill the 17/64-inch hole for the bottom pin on the midline centered 7/16 inch up from the bottom (hole #3). Drill this hole 2-1/4 inches deep. Enlarge the opening of this hole to 1/2 inch for a depth of 5/16 inch to hold the magnet and a plug over the magnet.

Now cut the groove for the top pin in the locking part of the hasp. With the hasp back in place in the lock body in the closed position, lightly mark the locking end where it exits the body. Again, entirely remove the hasp. Place a piece of 3/8-inch indexing dowel in the top hole of the lock body, and mark where it exits. With this dowel in place, drill a 17/64-inch hole 1/8 inch into the dowel, using the hole for the top pin as a guide. Place the dowel next to the locking end of the hasp so that the exit marks line up. Mark the hasp in the location corresponding with the hole in the index dowel and file a 3/16-inch deep groove on the inner surface of the hasp at this location. Sand the hasp and apply the finish.

Cut the four pins next. The top pin is approximately 3/4 inch long. The center pin is 1-7/16 inch long. Each of the bottom pins is 3/4 inch long. The end of the bottom pin that contacts the magnet is tapered and rounded to reduce the strength of attraction. Make sure all the pins are the proper length before assembly.

The "keyway" is made from a plug cut from layered light and dark wood. It fills the hole beneath the center pin of the padlock.

The plug that fills the hole to cover the end of the center pin is made to resemble a keyway. To make the plug, lightly mark a 1/2-inch circle on a 1/8-inch thick piece of light-colored wood such as cherry or maple. With the scroll saw, cut a keyway in the circle. Glue this piece of wood to a piece of 3/16-inch thick darker wood. This piece should be about 2 inches by 4 inches. When the glue dries, cut out the 1/2-inch circle with a plug cutter. Place the center pin in its hole and glue the keyway plug behind it.

Install the bottom pins. Put in a 1/2-inch by 3/16-inch disk magnet (ceramic, not rare earth, which is too strong), and plug the hole. Make the plug from a scrap of padlock wood so the grain matches; glue in place. After the glue dries, sand the plug flush with the body. Sand the entire lock body and finish. I like tung oil followed by gel polyurethane. To place the top pin, retract the center pin by tappping the lock body over the magnet to free the bottom pins and spin the body on its bottom. The center pin should fall. Slide in the top pin. Place the hasp in position and put a 3/16-inch steel pivot pin in place.

Here's how to lock the padlock. With the hasp closed, turn the lock on its side with the locking end of the hasp down. Continue turning the lock upside down, and gently shake so the bottom pins contact the magnet. To open the padlock, tap the lock over the magnet, sit the lock on its bottom and spin it, turn the lock on its side with the locking end of the hasp up, and pivot the hasp open.

"Heart and ?" Puzzle

This elegant box has a simple concealed locking mechanism. It can serve as a gift box for a ring or other trinket. Here is how it's made.

This lovely box uses four pins as part of its locking mechanism. The woods used in the box at left are mahogany and rosewood. The woods in the box at right are maple and padauk.

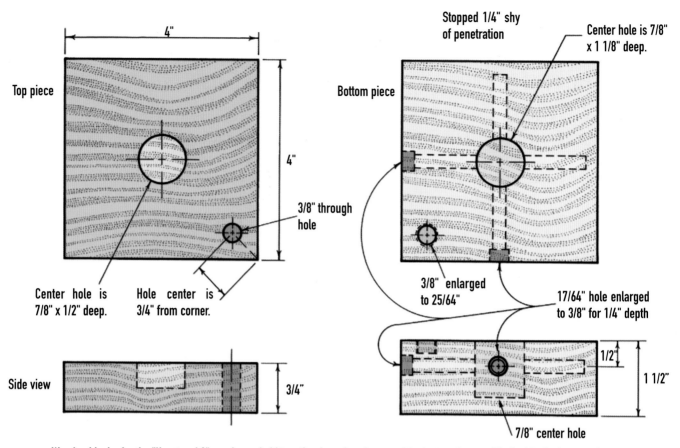

Top piece

4"

4"

3/8" through hole

Center hole is 7/8" x 1/2" deep.

Hole center is 3/4" from corner.

Side view

3/4"

Bottom piece

Stopped 1/4" shy of penetration

Center hole is 7/8" x 1 1/8" deep.

3/8" enlarged to 25/64"

17/64" hole enlarged to 3/8" for 1/4" depth

1/2"

1 1/2"

7/8" center hole

Wooden blocks for the "Heart and ?" puzzle are held together by a dowel secured to the top piece and locked in the bottom piece.

Start with two pieces of wood, each 4 inches by 4 inches. The bottom piece is 1-1/2 inches thick and the top is 3/4 inch thick. In the center of each piece, drill a 7/8-inch diameter hole. Drill the hole to a depth of 1-1/8 inches in the bottom and 1/2 inch deep in the top. Cut a 7/8-inch hardwood dowel 1-1/2 inches long and glue it into the hole in the top piece. After the glue dries, insert the dowel in the hole drilled in the bottom piece. It is important that the dowel move easily in the hole in the bottom piece. Lightly sand the dowel and hole if necessary. Align as well as possible the sides of the top and bottom. It's okay if they're slightly off at this point. Tape the pieces together.

Now drill a 3/8-inch hole centered 3/4 inch in from one corner. This hole should pass through the top piece and extend 1/4 inch into the bottom piece. It is for a dowel that will keep the top and bottom in alignment. Separate the top and bottom and enlarge the hole in the bottom piece to 25/64 inch. Cut a 1-inch length of 3/8-inch dowel and round one end slightly. Put the pieces back together and force this dowel through the hole in the top and into the bottom. Place a dab of glue on the dowel just before it reaches its full extent.

Top piece (side view)

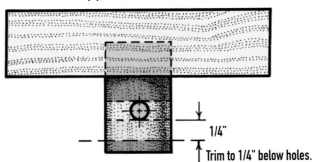

The center dowel is trimmed to 1/4" below the horizontal hole. The space between this dowel and the bottom of the hole in the heart is for a trinket.

1/4"

Trim to 1/4" below holes.

On two adjacent sides of the bottom piece, place marks in the center line 1/2 inch from the top edge. Drill a 17/64-inch hole to a depth of 3-3/4 inches into each of the marked sides—you will intersect the center dowel. Enlarge the two holes in the bottom piece to 3/8 inch for a depth of 1/4 inch. (These holes will be plugged later.) After this is done, remove the top piece and trim the 7/8-inch dowel so that it extends only about 1/4 inch below the hole. The space between the dowel and the bottom of the 7/8-inch center hole becomes the hiding spot for the trinket.

Cut four metal locking pins from 1/4-inch steel or brass rod, each 1-1/4 inch long. Test-fit them to be sure that when they are retracted in their holes they do not extend into the center 7/8-inch hole. Shorten them if necessary. Lightly round each end of the pins. Place two pins in each hole, plug the holes and sand the plugs flush. Push the four metal pins out of the center hole and put the top piece in place. Gently shake the piece so that the pins slide into the center dowel. This locks the puzzle. All four pins will not retract entirely unless the puzzle is spun.

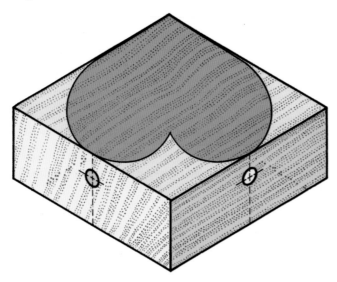

Draw an outline of the heart on the wood block. Areas overlying holes and plugs are indicated— minimal material will be removed here.

Draw the heart outline on either the top or bottom piece. Remember that there is only 1/4 inch of wood overlying the ends of the holes containing the pins. The edges of the heart need to approximate the edges of the square in those locations. Cut out the heart. I like to round over both top and bottom edges of the assembled heart with a 1/4-inch radius or larger round-over bit. Sand the puzzle smooth. After sanding, finish with a penetrating oil and wipe-on polyurethane.

Spinning the puzzle allows the top piece to be lifted off. As mentioned, the centrifugal force pulls the pins out of the center dowel. To work properly, the center of gravity should be at the middle of the 7/8-inch dowel. The puzzle should balance on a small dowel placed under this point. It may be necessary to sand excess material from the heart so that this is possible.

"The Bolt (To Drive You Nuts!)"

This puzzle has a two-stage locking mechanism consisting of two locking horizontal pins and a screw in a keyhole slot.

When assembled, this puzzle makes an attractive decoration, and it's great fun to play with. There are two wooden parts, the shaft and the head—the object is to remove the head to find the nut hidden inside the shaft.

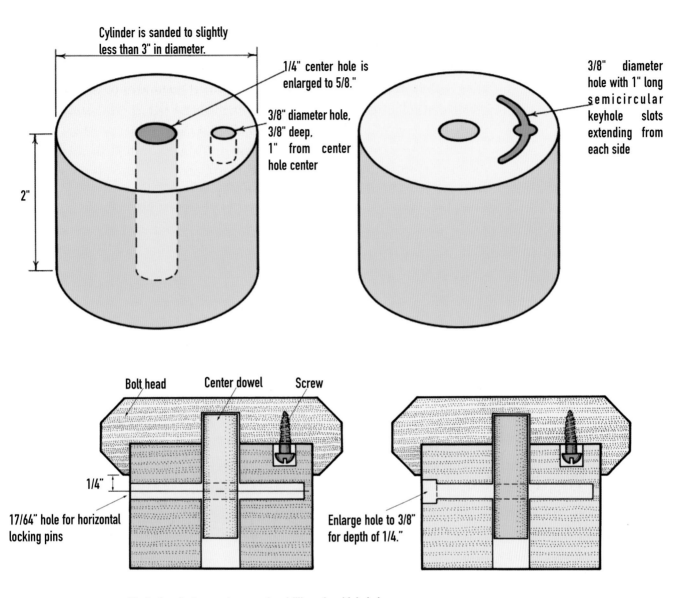

Cylinder is sanded to slightly less than 3" in diameter.

1/4" center hole is enlarged to 5/8."

3/8" diameter hole, 3/8" deep. 1" from center hole center

2"

3/8" diameter hole with 1" long semicircular keyhole slots extending from each side

Bolt head Center dowel Screw

1/4"

17/64" hole for horizontal locking pins

Enlarge hole to 3/8" for depth of 1/4."

The lock cylinder requires precise drilling of multiple holes.

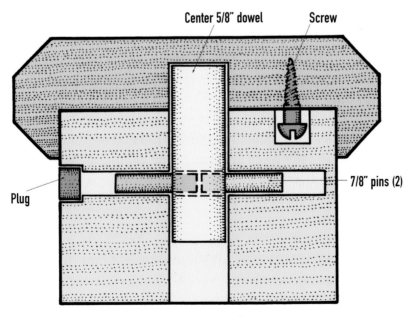

Center 5/8" dowel Screw

Plug

7/8" pins (2)

Bolt showing pins engaging center dowel

Make the threaded shaft from a 3-inch-diameter cylinder that is 3-3/4 inches long. I use a 3-1/4-inch hole saw, which can cut a cylinder 2 inches thick, so I cut two cylinders from 2-inch thick wood and glue them together later. Both cylinders must be reduced to a final diameter of slightly less than 3 inches (so that the cylinder will easily turn in the 3-inch hole in the bolt head). This is accomplished by sanding them as they are turned on the drill press, just as was done with the disks for the lighthouse ball maze.

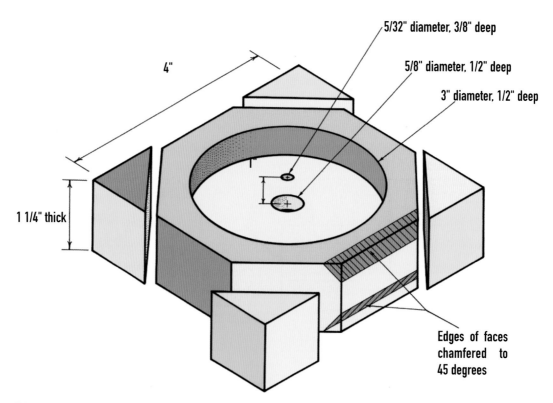

This drawing of the bolt head shows the location of the holes. The edges of all eight sides are chamfered to 45 degrees.

The bolt head is made from a 4-inch by 4-inch, 1-1/4-inch thick piece of wood that either matches or contrasts with the wood used for the shaft. To make the head, drill a 3-inch diameter hole to a depth of 1/2 inch in the center of the piece. Cut off the corners of the square to make an octagon. Chamfer the top and bottom edges of each side of the octagon to 45 degrees. In the center of the 3-inch hole, drill a 5/8-inch diameter hole that is 1/2 inch deep. Also drill a 5/32-inch diameter hole that is 3/8 inch deep—position it 1 inch from the center of the 5/8-inch hole. Glue a 2-inch long piece of 5/8-inch dowel into the center hole. Screw a brass #10-3/4-inch round-head screw into the 5/32-inch hole so that slightly less than 3/8 inch of its length extends above the hole.

The locking mechanism is machined into one of the two 3-inch diameter cylinders. Enlarge the center 1/4-inch hole to 5/8 inch for its entire length. Drill a 3/8-inch diameter hole, 3/8 inch deep, 1 inch from the center of what will be called the top of the cylinder from now on.

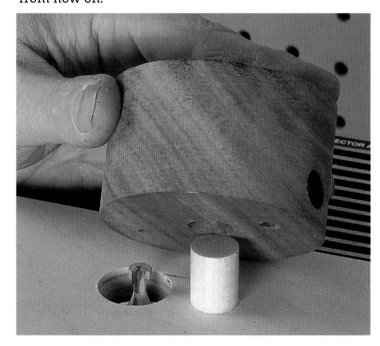

Lowering the bolt-shaft disk onto the keyhole slot cutter is made more accurate and safer when you use a plywood fixture.

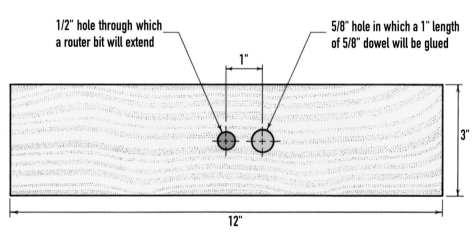

The fixture to create a semicircular keyhole slot is made from 1/4-inch thick plywood.

The next operation is cutting the semicircular keyhole slots on each side of the 3/8-inch diameter hole. For this you will need to make a fixture for the router table. Drill a 1/2-inch hole in the center of a 3-inch by 12-inch piece of 1/4-inch thick plywood. Drill a 5/8-inch diameter hole in the midline centered 1 inch from the center of the 1/2-inch hole. Glue a 1-inch length of 5/8-inch diameter dowel in the 5/8-inch hole. Place the fixture on the router table and raise a 3/8-inch diameter keyhole router bit through the exact center of the 1/2-inch hole and clamp the fixture to the table. Adjust the height of the bit so its top is 3/8 inch above the fixture.

With the router turned on, place the cylinder on the dowel of the fixture, positioned so that the router bit enters the 3/8-inch hole already drilled in the cylinder. Holding the cylinder tightly, push it flat on the fixture, and rotate it 1 inch clockwise, back to the starting place, and 1 inch counterclockwise. Turn off the router and remove the cylinder from the fixture. Place the bolt head on the cylinder so that the center dowel enters the center hole in the cylinder, and the screw head enters the hole in the center of the keyway slot. Make sure that the plug turns freely through the full extent of the keyway slot. If it does, turn the head clockwise, to its furthest extent, and tape the two pieces in this position.

A cradle fixture stabilizes the plug during drilling.

Next, drill the hole for the horizontal locking pins. To stabilize the cylinder while drilling, I use a cradle fixture. Make the cradle from a 4-inch by 4-inch piece of 2-inch thick wood. Drill a 3-inch hole in the wood and cut the piece in half through the center of the hole, parallel to one of the sides.

Drill a 17/64-inch hole into the side of the cylinder, centered 1/4 inch below the bottom of the bolt head. This hole will penetrate through the center dowel. Drill it to a depth of 2-3/4 inches. Remove the bolt head from the cylinder and trim the center dowel so it extends about 1/2 inch below the hole for the horizontal pins.

Make two horizontal pins, each 7/8 inch long, out of 1/4-inch steel or brass rod. Place the bolt head on the cylinder and turn it to the locked position. Place the pins in the hole. The pins should be able to slide back and forth through the center dowel. Plug the hole behind these pins with a plug cut from the offcut of the cylinder wood, matching the grain. Trim and sand the plug to match the profile of the cylinder. The puzzle is locked by one or both pins extending from the cylinder into the center dowel. Place the cylinder and head upright and spin it to retract the pins. Twist the bolt head until the screw aligns with the hole in the key slot and remove.

Now glue the second 3-inch diameter cylinder on the bottom of the machined cylinder after aligning the grain patterns of the two pieces. This creates the bolt shaft. When the glue dries, you can cut the faux threads in the shaft. The first groove between the threads is cut at the edge of the joint between the two cylinders. Raise the blade on your table saw to 1/8 inch. Move the rip fence to 2 inches from the blade. Holding the top of the bolt shaft against the fence, roll the shaft over the spinning blade to create a 1/8-inch deep kerf around the entire circumference of the cylinder. Cut the other threads using the thread cutter as shown.

Cut the "threads" on the bolt shaft on a table saw using a simple thread-cutting fixture.

Start making the thread cutter fixture by mounting a two-piece cradle on a piece of 1/4-inch plywood. Make the cradle by cutting in half a 2-inch thick, 3-1/2-inch square of wood with a 3-inch hole in its center. On the side of one of the cradle pieces, glue the "thread follower." Make the thread follower by cutting a 1/8-inch slice off a 3-1/2-inch square of wood that has had a 2-3/4-inch hole drilled in its center. This 1/8-inch slice is cut in half and one half is glued on the cradle. The thread follower extends 1/8 inch proud of the cradle.

Glue the cradle pieces 1 inch apart in the midline of an 8-inch by 12-inch piece of plywood. Clamp the plywood sheet on the saw in the cradle perpendicular to the blade. The highest point of the blade should be in the midline of the cradle. In addition, when the blade is raised between the cradles, it should be 1/8 inch away from the thread follower. With the saw running, raise the blade to cut into the plywood. The height of the blade when cutting the grooves between the threads should be equal to the height of the thread follower.

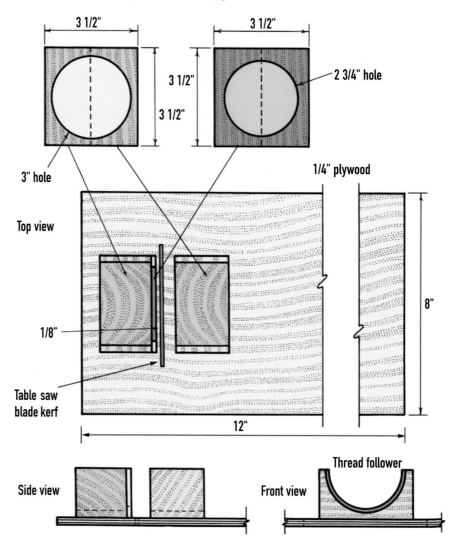

This fixture will help you cut faux threads safely and accurately.

In this photo, the pencil points to the thread follower.

Roll the kerf already cut in the bolt shaft on the thread follower with the blade turning, creating a 1/8-inch thread. Move the shaft as necessary to cut faux threads from about 1-1/4 inches from the top of the shaft to the bottom. After cutting the threads, trim the shaft to a final length of about 3-3/4 inches—the bottom ends with a band of shaft body.

Trim the bolt shaft so that there is a full section of the body below the last "thread."

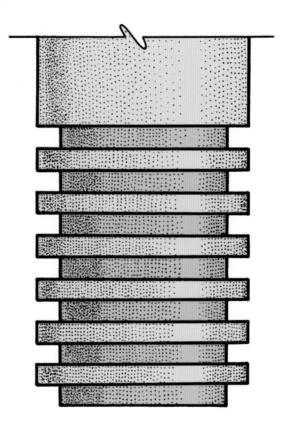

Glue a 1/4-inch plug in the hole in the bottom of the shaft. Sand and finish the bolt. Typically I use tung oil followed by three coats of brush-on oil-based polyurethane for this puzzle (you'll need a brush to get into the groove between the threads).

Hexagonal Dovetail Puzzle

This is the puzzle that first appeared in *American Woodworker* magazine (August 1998). In a way, it's the puzzle that is responsible for this book, as I mentioned in the Introduction. It's challenging to make and open, and since the hexagon has a dovetail on each face, how it will open becomes even more mysterious. These dovetails connect the top and bottom. The top is prevented from sliding off by a locking mechanism with three components. Therefore, it takes three separate actions to open the locked puzzle, as we shall see.

The object of this puzzle is to get to the penny hidden inside. The puzzles are made of mahogany, maple, and rosewood (right), and black walnut, maple, and purpleheart (left).

The wooden part of the puzzle is made from three pieces of clear hardwood, a 1-inch thick piece and a 3/4-inch thick piece glued together to make the top, and a 2-inch thick piece for the bottom. Use contrasting woods to make the puzzle more attractive. The two pieces into which the dovetail pins and grooves are cut are oriented so that the pins and grooves run across the grain.

After gluing together the parts for the top, cut the top and bottom to 4 inches by 4 inches. Cut the three dovetail pins in the bottom with a 14-degree dovetail bit on the router table. (Remove much of the waste first with the table saw by kerfing to 7/16 inch deep.) Rout the mating grooves in the top after removing waste with the table saw. Set the groove locations on the router table using the bottom piece as a guide. After the grooves are cut, slide the pieces together. They should fit well and slide smoothly. If they do, tape them together, then cut the top and bottom to final front-to-back depth (3-7/16 inches). Cut off a slice slightly thicker than 3/8 inch from what will become the front of the puzzle and the rest from the back. Because the offcut from the front will be used to make a plug, mark it and its previous location so you can match the grain later.

Three pieces of wood are used to make the hexagonal dovetail puzzle.

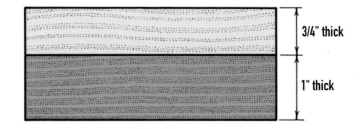

3/4" thick

1" thick

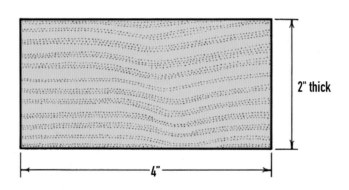

2" thick

4"

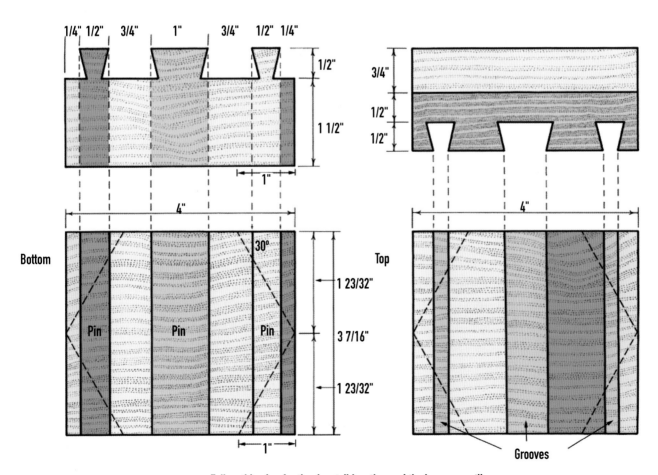

Follow this plan for the dovetail location and the hexagon outline.

Your top and bottom now measure 4 inches by 3-7/16 inches. With the table saw (or, more easily, with a radial arm saw or sliding miter saw) make the 30-degree cuts 1 inch from each side (measured on the 4 inch width.) These cuts will result in a hexagon that measures 2 inches on a side; each side has a 1-inch dovetail centered on it. Drill two 1/4-inch holes in the front of the puzzle—one in the pin and one just above it. Plug these holes—they serve as alignment markers.

Top

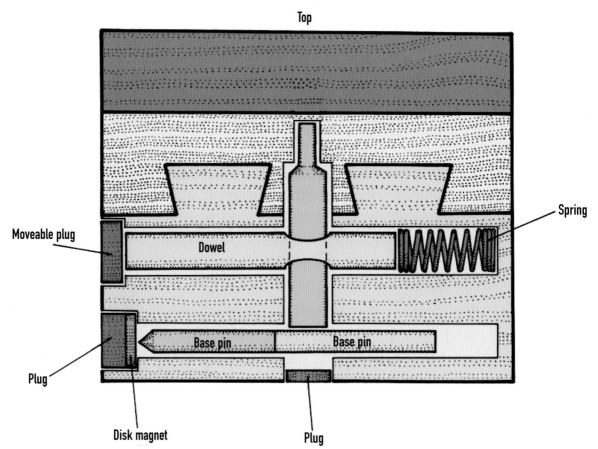

Moveable plug

Dowel

Spring

Plug

Base pin

Base pin

Disk magnet

Plug

The locking mechanism features a spring-loaded dowel to stabilize the center locking post, as well as a magnetic catch.

The next operation is drilling the holes for the locking mechanism. Check that the top and bottom pieces are taped together in perfect alignment. Then, in the exact center of the bottom of the bottom piece, drill a 3/16-inch hole to a depth of 2-1/2 inches. Enlarge this hole to a diameter of 17/64 inch to a depth of 1-3/4 inches measured from the surface. Enlarge this hole again to 3/8 inch for a depth of 1/8 inch. This stepped hole is the hole for the center locking post.

Turn the puzzle on one of its sides—not the back or front. On the "up" side, drill a 17/64-inch hole 3-1/4 inches deep from the surface, centered 1/2 inch up from the bottom edge in the midline. Enlarge it to 1/2 inch for a depth of 3/8 inch. This hole must precisely intersect the hole for the center locking post. It will accommodate the base pins and a magnet, which keeps the pins from moving unintentionally.

Finally, drill the hole for the spring-loaded dowel that stabilizes the center locking post. In the center of the front face of the bottom, drill a 1/2-inch hole 3-1/8 inches deep measured from the surface of the face. Enlarge this hole to 3/4 inch for 3/8 inches in depth. Locate this hole so it's centered on and perpendicular to the center post hole.

The locking components—the steel rod pieces and the spring-loaded dowel—are machined next. The center locking post is made from a 1-3/4-inch length of 1/4-inch-diameter steel rod (brass rod also works well). One end of the rod is reduced to a diameter of slightly less than 3/16 inch for a distance of 5/8 inch. This can be done using a file while turning the rod in the drill press. Use a circle of plastic from a nut can top taped on the chuck to protect the chuck while filing. Cut two base pins from 1/4-inch steel rod, each 1-1/4 inch long. Taper the end of the pin that will contact the magnet to a rounded point to decrease the force of attraction between the magnet and the pin. Smooth the ends of both pins and the center post so they'll slide freely in their respective holes.

Now drill the spring-loaded dowel. Cut a 4-inch length of 1/2-inch hardwood dowel and sand it lightly so that it slides easily in the 1/2-inch hole in the front face of the bottom. Stabilize it in its hole and drill a 17/64-inch hole through the dowel, using the hole for the center locking post as a guide. Mark the dowel's orientation and remove it, then enlarge the hole slightly with a round file or sandpaper wrapped around a nail. Cut the end of the dowel that extends toward the back of the puzzle to 7/8 inch long, measured from the hole center to the end. Cut the end that extends toward the front to 1-3/8 inch from the hole center.

Assembly of the parts proceeds as follows: Place a 7/16-inch by 1-inch spring in the 1/2-inch hole, followed by the machined dowel. Align the hole in the dowel with the center hole and drop in the center locking post. Be sure that the dowel, when pushed against the center post by the spring, extends into the 3/4-inch hole in the front face about 1/16 inch. Trim if necessary. Cut a 3/4-inch plug from the offcut you've been saving and glue it to the front end of the dowel. Try to match the grain of the plug with the front face and be careful that no glue gets on the sides of the plug or in the hole. Place the two base pins in the bottom hole, oriented so that the rounded point of the one pin is pointing toward the entry hole—and the magnet. Force a 1/2-inch by 3/16-inch disk magnet into the entry hole and fill the hole with a plug cut from the offcut of the original bottom piece. After the glue completely dries, sand all the plugs flush with the puzzle surfaces. Chamfer the edges of the top of the puzzle to 45 degrees.

Ease the bottom and side corners of the puzzle and the sharp edges of the dovetails. Take special care that sawdust doesn't enter the hole for the center post, since it will gum up the works.

Drill a 3/4-inch hole in the top of the center dovetail pin to a depth of 1/8 inch to hold a penny. Finish the exterior of the puzzle, and wax the pins and grooves of the sliding dovetails.

This is how to operate the puzzle: Hit the puzzle over the magnet to knock the base pins free, set the puzzle on a flat surface and spin it to separate the base pins, and push the plug on the front face to allow the center post to retract into the bottom. The top can then be slid off, revealing the penny. To lock the puzzle, align the top and bottom, turn the puzzle upside down, and push the front plug to allow the center post to drop into place. Jiggle the puzzle to allow the base pins to contact the magnet and each other.

Appendix: Workshop injuries

When I was about ten years old, my Dad made a decorative crosscut on his thumb with his table saw. Of all the things that he demonstrated to me in his shop, this was probably the most valuable. If my Dad, who I considered an intelligent, conscientious woodworker, could injure himself like this, anyone could. I keep this thought in mind whenever I turn on a power tool.

In my career as a physician, I have seen and treated a number of workshop injuries, some major, but, fortunately, most minor. My reason for including information about injuries in this book is certainly not to dissuade anyone from woodworking. Rather, I want to drive home the point that accidents can and do happen. Complacency can be hazardous to your health.

To begin this section on a lighter note, let me tell you a story that I recently heard. It seems that there was a doctor who, when sitting in his office, was constantly bothered by some oak trim around one of the windows that just didn't fit right. Finally, able to tolerate it no longer, he called a finish carpenter to come and replace the trim. The finish carpenter arrived, set to work replacing the trim with perfectly mitered pieces, and completed his work in about fifteen minutes. When the carpenter presented the doctor a bill with a labor charge of $150, the doctor remarked, "$150 for fifteen minutes' work...I don't even make that much!" The carpenter replied, "I didn't either when I was a doctor."

Eye injuries

Statistically, accidents involving the eye are the most common injuries in the workshop. Fortunately, they are usually not serious. Still, it is just good common sense to wear safety glasses, goggles, face shields and other appropriate eye protection in the shop.

The typical pattern of eye injuries is that sawdust or fine wood chips are blown into the eye and washed out by flowing tears. However, more serious injuries can occur, and if they're not handled properly, even minor occurrences can have significant consequences. This is especially true if metal or a small bit of abrasive gets into the eye. Sharp, hard objects can scratch the eye surface or penetrate the outer layer. Certain material may also cause an allergic or other inflammatory reaction.

If anything gets in the eye, the first step is rinsing, preferably with commercial saline (dilute salt water). Never try to rub foreign matter out of your eye. Look in a mirror to define the extent of the injury. This may be difficult, because when the eye is irritated, the muscles of protection around the eye cause squinting. If there is a small object that moves with each blink, use the corner of a clean rag or cotton swab to try to get it out, or have someone else do it. Do not use a finger. If there's a fleck or a glint of reflected light that does not seem to move on the surface of the eye, the fragment may have penetrated. Penetrations require medical attention. This is especially true if the foreign matter is ferrous metal because, if not removed in a timely fashion, a "rust ring" may form in the tissue around the fragment. A rust ring can cause distortion to the vision or lead to further damage to the eye by ulcer formation.

Scratches of the outer surface of the eye usually heal—fairly rapidly—without consequence. But scratches can be painful and become infected. If after getting something in the eye it becomes increasingly red, painful, or swollen, or if pus forms, vision blurs, headaches develop, or things just don't seem right, get your eye checked out. Eyes are too valuable to risk.

Abrasions, lacerations, and amputations

Woodworkers routinely handle sharp and rough things and the skin doesn't provide a very tough barrier to penetration. Breaks in the skin can range from insignificant to extremely serious. I've read that over 700,000 arm and hand injuries resulting from home-building products occur each year.

In spite of my consciousness of injury, I have had a few mishaps myself. I ran the tip of my left thumb into the band saw when reaching for a small offcut. I sanded off a small area of skin from my right index finger with a bench-top sander when a small piece of wood I was holding slipped away. And, ironically, I had a table-saw injury while working on an article on table-saw injuries for *American Woodworker* magazine. As I was cutting a wedge off an 8/4 piece of black walnut, the wedge fell between the blade and the throat plate. The wedge forced the blade against the plate, knocking off two carbide teeth. One tooth embedded itself in my right arm. It came out easily and did not require additional attention other than a tetanus booster. Accidents can happen!

If you happen to become injured in the workshop, remain calm. This can be more difficult to do than it sounds, since it's natural to experience a variety of emotions—including panic. Once you compose yourself, turn off the tool. Assess your injury, or ask somebody else to. If there is bleeding, apply direct pressure with a piece of gauze or a clean rag.

If the wound is superficial, you can probably handle it at home. Clean the wound with mild soap and water and cover it with a bandage or gauze and tape to keep dirt out. An over-the-counter antibiotic ointment from the pharmacy may speed healing. I cover superficial injuries with gel cyanoacrylate, otherwise known as Superglue, Krazy Glue, and Permabond, among other brands.

I first read about using gel cyanoacrylate on skin in the dermatology literature, which reported that it made a good cover for those nasty little skin cracks that can form around finger joints, especially in wintertime. I have subsequently found many additional references for its safe use in the medical literature. Over-the-counter glues contain methyl or ethyl cyanoacrylate. This substance may be more toxic than butyl cyanoacrylate, which is available in Canada and Europe, and octyl cyanoacrylate, which is related to Super Glue. Octyl cyanoacrylate has been approved by the FDA for use in closing certain

---

Injury Statistics

In 1987, *The Journal of Hand Surgery* discussed data reported from a survey published by *Fine Woodworking* magazine in 1983. Readers who had sustained "a serious injury involving loss of fingers or parts of fingers, or hand wounds that required care at a hospital or doctor's office" were asked to complete a questionnaire. There were 1,002 responses out of a reported magazine circulation of 230,000. Here are some of the interesting findings:

60.5% of the respondents considered themselves amateurs.

Table saws were involved with 42% of the injuries.

Jointers, although considered the most potentially dangerous tool by respondents, caused 18% of the total injuries.

37% of respondents had amputated one or more digits. Table saws and jointers were involved in 78% of amputations.

The most common cause of injury reported was failure to use appropriate blade guards.

The second highest cause of injury reported resulted from performance of an "intrinsically dangerous" operation.

Since the time of day during which injuries occurred was reported, afternoon (after lunch) tiredness was thought to contribute to risk.

types of wounds, but at this time it is available for use only by physicians. All cyanoacrylates form a moisture-resistant barrier with some antibacterial properties. I have found that gel cyanoacrylates don't sting or burn, and actually ease pain. If you read the label on these glues, you'll find warnings about inhaling the fumes and getting the product in eyes. Heed them. In addition, it is possible—although extremely rare—for people to be allergic to gel cyanoacrylates. If you find you experience redness of the skin, hives, nasal congestion, breathing difficulties, headache, blurred vision, or any other reaction, obviously you shouldn't use the products.

Back to wound evaluation—if the wound is bad, get medical attention. How do you know if a wound is "bad"? Use these characteristics to judge:

• The laceration is longer than 1 inch and/or approximately deeper than 1/4 inch.

• It is close to a joint.

• It involves bone, as would be fairly obvious from its location.

• It is accompanied by loss of feeling or inability to move nearby joints or body parts, like fingers.

• It is hard to close or keep closed with a simple bandage, and bleeding cannot be controlled.

• It might leave an unattractive scar in a visible location.

• Dirt, wood, metal fragments, or other debris cannot easily be washed out.

• The wound is a puncture, especially in the sole of the foot or palm of the hand

• Your tetanus immunity needs boosting (more on tetanus later in this chapter).

This being said, if any wound starts to show increasing warmth, spreading redness (especially in linear streaks), swelling, pus, or if a fever develops, seek medical attention without delay. This is especially true with finger and hand injuries because of the possibility of the rapid spread of an infection.

Sadly, amputations are not uncommon workshop injuries. Initial treatment of an amputation is the same as for other serious lacerations, but care needs to be given to the severed part as well. After controlling bleeding with direct pressure, find the severed part, wrap it in some saline-soaked gauze, place it in a small plastic bag, and place this bag in a larger container with ice or a chemical cold pack. A part that is cared for in this way stands the best chance of being reattached or used for graft material.

One more consideration when dealing with workshop injuries: If you're feeling lightheaded or dizzy, don't hesitate to call for help, including dialing 911. People suffering from a hand injury commonly feel nauseated, lightheaded, or even pass out, and it's better to be driven to the appropriate medical facility than to have a car accident on your way there.

Tetanus

Tetanus, also called lockjaw, is a nasty disease caused by the Clostridium tetani bacteria. This bacteria lives in the intestinal tract of many animals. The organism forms a spore (a non-vegetative, protective, capsule-like form), that allows it to lie dormant in soil. When conditions for life are appropriate, the spore changes into a vegetative form capable of metabolism and reproduction. The bacteria produces a protein that is one of the two most potent toxins known—tetanospasmin. (The other potent toxin is the one that causes botulism.) When this toxin enters the human body, it causes muscles to contract and spasm. Frequently, one of the first muscles affected is the one that closes the jaw, hence the term "lockjaw." In the United States, cases are still reported every year, although they number fewer than ten.

An acidic, oxygen-free environment—such as found in an infected wound—is required for tetanus to thrive. While puncture wounds from rusty nails are typically associated with tetanus, even apparently insignificant wounds have been related to this disease.

The best defense against tetanus is active immunization. In this country most children are protected by mandated immunizations during the first few months of life and prior to starting school. Adults are more likely at risk, especially if boosters are not obtained every ten years. Suffice it to say that woodworkers should make it a point to keep their tetanus immunity up to date. In general, if you've had a booster within the last

---

Shop First-Aid Kit

Every shop should have a well-stocked first-aid kit on hand. Replenish supplies as you use them. The kit should contain:

10 assorted bandages

5 gauze dressings (known as 4x4s)

1 long dressing gauze strip (known as Kerlex or Kling)

1 roll of adhesive tape

1 3" elastic bandage

1 pair of latex gloves

1 squeeze bottle of sterile saline

1 small mirror

1 splinter forceps (tweezers with a fine point)

1 magnifying lens

1 tube of gel cyanoacrylate (Super Glue or other brand)

plastic bags, 1 small and 1 large

1 chemical cold pack

index card with the date of your last tetanus booster

index card with phone numbers of your physician, nearest emergency room, and ambulance.

ten years and you get a clean wound, you should be protected. If the wound is dirty, a booster within the last five years should be okay. If the wound presents significant risk of tetanus, your doctor may decide to administer a dose of tetanus immune globulin, which conveys immediate protection against the disease.

Splinters

Small pieces of wood that penetrate the skin are a frequent annoyance in the workshop. Remove them as quickly as possible with tweezers. The longer a splinter remains, the more extractives can leech into the tissue, increasing the risk of an inflammatory or allergic reaction. Also, splinters can increase the risk of infection.

Burns

Thermal burns in most workshops are infrequent and typically of the superficial, first-degree type. They usually occur when a woodworker grabs something hot, such as a drill bit that has just been whirring in hardwood or metal. Burns that don't destroy the skin or other tissues are usually not dangerous, just painful, because the irritation in the burn area causes pain-transmitting substances to be released. Abrasions, such as caused by rapidly moving sandpaper, are similar to thermal burns. The best—and usually only—treatment needed is immediate cooling of the burn with ice or cold water. This stops the cascade of inflammation during which the pain transmitters are released. If blisters do form, as in a second-degree burn, watch them for signs of secondary infection. Redness, red streaks, or pus all signal the need for an immediate trip to your physician.

Burns caused by chemicals such as caustic paint strippers are easily avoided by wearing rubber gloves, protective clothing, and a face shield. If a chemical spatters on skin or in eyes, follow directions on the container. Know what to do ahead of time so you can act fast if you need to.

Irritations and allergic reactions

Both vapors and solids, such as wood dust, can cause reactions ranging from insignificant (sneezing) to serious (asthma). An excellent summary—Woodworking Hazards by Michael McCann and Angela Babin—can be found on the Internet at *www.unco.edu/safety/woodworkhaz.htm.*

Harmful vapors can be released from a variety of materials, such as epoxy hardeners, solvents, adhesives, paint strippers, and wood finishes. Even the act of machining plywood releases formaldehyde, which can spur a reaction in some people. Good ventilation as provided by open windows and/or window fans can take care of most risks, but be on the alert for signs of allergy: runny nose; itchy, tearing, or burning eyes; coughing; headache; and skin redness or itchiness. People who smoke, have other allergies (especially the respiratory type), or respiratory diseases need to be particularly careful. NIOSH-approved respirators with organic vapor cartridges are available and will protect against most of these hazardous vapors, but their use is rarely necessary in the home environment.

Many wood species, including domestic woods such as oak and willow as well as tropical woods such as African blackwood, can contain allergy-producing oils and resins. Dust from these woods can provoke severe reactions in sensitive people, and frequent exposure over many years has even been linked to certain types of cancer. Exposure to wood dust can be significantly reduced by properly installed and functioning dust collectors and air filters. Dust-filter masks are a good idea, especially when working with woods to which one is sensitive. From personal experience, I find I can avoid coughing and sneezing by wearing a mask when working with padauk and rosewood. NIOSH-approved particulate masks, typically having double elastic straps, provide the best protection. There are multiple suppliers of NIOSH-approved respirators and masks located on the internet. You can also usually find advertisements from companies selling these products in woodworking magazines.

Vibration injuries and hearing loss

Over time, the frequent use of vibrating hand tools can lead to loss of sensation and possible bone and soft tissue damage in the hands. Carpal tunnel syndrome can result from vibration or repetitive motion. Although not a significant problem for the casual woodworker, it's a good idea to wear gloves while using vibrating hand

93

tools. Should you start to experience pain or numbness and tingling of the thumb and first two fingers, consider wearing a wrist brace.

Since many woodshop tools are loud and their continued use can eventually lead to hearing loss, it makes sense to wear earplugs and/or "muffs" in the shop. To lower noise levels, keep your machines tuned and well lubricated, and invest in anti-vibration pads to place under your machines.

Strains and sprains

Sprains and strains can happen in the workshop just like in the rest of the world. Consider this scenario: You step over a board on the floor only to land on a small piece of dowel. The resulting ankle twist and possible fall might result in a sprained ankle or strained knee. By definition, a sprain is a stretch of the ligaments holding bones together at a joint; a strain is a pull on muscles or their tendons. Assuming no fractures, and sometimes x-rays are necessary to reveal fractures, the best treatment is ice, rest, elevation of the injured part, and external pressure, such as an elastic bandage, to keep down swelling. Over-the-counter pain medications, such as acetaminophen, will help. Symptoms that suggest a trip to the doctor include the inability to bear weight on the injured joint, intense or persistent pain, and significant swelling or discoloration.

Appendix: Bibliography

Coffin, Stewart T., 1992. *Puzzle Craft*. Lincoln, MA: self-published, copies available through *www.johnrausch.com*.

Dresdner, Michael, 1999. *The New Wood Finishing Book*. Newtown, CT: The Taunton Press.

Farhi, Sivy, 1982. *Soma World – the Complete Soma Cube*, self-published, available on some internet puzzle sites. Hard to find but worth the hunt.

Forest Products Laboratory, 1999. *Wood handbook: Wood as an Engineering Material, General Technical Report FPL-GTR-113*. Madison, WI: U.S. Department of Agriculture, Forest Service, Forest Products Laboratory.

Golomb, Solomon W., 1994. *Polyominoes*. Princeton, NJ: Princeton University Press.

Hoadley, R. Bruce, 1980. *Understanding Wood: A Craftsman's Guide to Wood Technology*. Newtown, CT: The Taunton Press.

Slocum, Jerry and Botermans, Jack, 1986. *Puzzles Old & New*. Seattle, WA: University of Washington Press. Out of print.

Young, William Tandy, 1998. *The Glue Book*. Newtown, CT: The Taunton Press.

Websites of interest to puzzle makers

PENTOMINOES
www.lonestar.texas.net/~jenicek/pentomin/pentomin.html

GENERAL PUZZLE MAKING
www.cleverwood.com
www.johnrausch.com
www.woodpuzzles.com
www.puzzlemuseum.com

Produced by Kelsey Editorial Services, Bethel, CT

Editor: Laura Tringali

Production Associate: Bran Chapman

Designer: Peggy Bloomer

Illustrator: Jim Goold

Photographer: Bob Mescavage

Printed by Khai Wah-Ferco Pte. Ltd., Singapore